# How to be an Outstanding Primary School Teacher

*Outstanding Teaching series*

DAVID DUNN

B L O O M S B U R Y
LONDON • NEW DELHI • NEW YORK • SYDNEY

Published 2012 by Bloomsbury

Bloomsbury Publishing plc
50 Bedford Square, London, WC1B 3DP
175 Fifth Avenue, New York, NY 10010

www.bloomsbury.com

ISBN: 978-1-4411-3841-5

First published in 2011 by Continuum, an imprint of Bloomsbury Publishing Plc

© David Dunn 2011

Typeset by Fakenham Prepress Solutions, Fakenham, Norfolk NR21 8NN
Printed and bound in Great Britain

# Contents

To my wife Sarah: thank you for all your help in making this possible.

# Introduction

Want to produce outstanding lessons on a regular basis? Want the children in your class to become fantastic learners, ready for anything that can be thrown at them? Want to have an absolute plethora of gold-standard, nailed-on, guaranteed-to-work-on-a-day-to-day-basis, easy-to-implement strategies to take your teaching (and your children's learning) to the next level? Well, they're all here! Let's face it, we all would like the mantle of 'Outstanding'; be that from the Head, our children, or, because you know you can't escape from them no matter how far you run, those dreaded OFSTED inspectors. This book won't give you all the answers, as teaching is a very complex practice, with no two lessons, or teachers, being the same. However, what you will find in this book is a multitude of ideas and strategies that have worked for me time and again, dispelling, along the way, the myths around:

◆ planning (no need to write down every word you're going to say)
◆ personalized learning (you will *not* have to plan for every individual child)
◆ Assessment for Learning (don't worry, we won't be looking at endless folders of statements)
◆ differentiation (yes, it is possible with very little extra work)
◆ questioning strategies (yes, *I know* you've probably done endless training on how to question – Bloom's Taxonomy anyone? But this is different); and a whole range of other tricks and tips across the entire gamut of teaching in the classroom strategies, guaranteed, if you invest the (relatively small) amount of time needed, to crash through the barrier of SATISFACTORY, beyond the (perfectly acceptable but oh-so-close-but-not-quite-there) category of GOOD, and fly, kicking and screaming, into where we all want to live – OUTSTANDING.

So how (I hear you ask) are we going to get there, and are we doing this just for the monster that is the lesson observation? In answer to the second question, a resounding *no*! And in answer to the first, *relatively easily*! Everything included in this book is proven classroom practice – it all works! However, please don't think this book will automatically make you an outstanding teacher; it won't, not without a little work on your part. There is a philosophy which underpins every strategy which you need to follow; it won't 'happen' just because you've read this book! However fantastic the ideas are in here, they will not work properly if you just try to 'do' them. However, follow the strategies and ideas alongside the correct philosophy and anything is possible!

Please be aware, though, this does come with a warning attached: you will become an outstanding teacher ... ALL THE TIME! (well, most of the time, anyway). This is *not* a do-this-and-you-may-get-an-outstanding-in-an-observation book; you will, of course, but these strategies will be so embedded, so the everyday norm will be that you will find yourself delivering outstanding lessons day after day. And when those dreaded observations are announced, you won't have to spend hours the night before stressing and re-writing your lesson plans; what you do from day to day will be what you do in your observation ... and the plaudits from those who have the power (in their world anyway) will follow swiftly behind.

There are many reasons why you might have bought this book, from worries about OFSTED to looming observations by your Senior Leadership Team. Or maybe you've bought this book because you just want to be better at certain aspects of your teaching – for example, Assessment for Learning or differentiation. Whatever the reason, this book will work for you in whatever way you wish to use it. Want to read it from cover to cover and get the whole 'Outstanding' experience? No problem. Want to dip in and out of particular areas of interest? Works great too. This book is designed to work with how *you* work; whatever works best for you works best! Even the most innovative, creative, fantastic of us need a little inspiration from time to time. And this book, however you decide to use it, will provide that. Or that's the plan.

So, on with the show.

# 1 The Outstanding Teacher ... Released!

Each of you has the potential to be an outstanding teacher. Fact. The fact you've bought this book indicates that you *want* to improve your practice, so you're well on the road to getting there! So, what is outstanding teaching? This question can be, and will be debated on and on. One thing we can say though (and this is agreed by everyone): for a lesson to be outstanding, there must be excellent outcomes. In other words, all the children need to have made significant progress. That's a tall order in itself, but not one that is insurmountable. So, are we talking about the outstanding *teacher*, or outstanding *teaching*? I think it is better to focus on how we can ensure that there is outstanding learning going on, which will mean that the teaching has been outstanding and, by default, the teacher is outstanding too. After all, it's the learning that really matters. When being observed, the observer will be looking for how much the children are learning: how much progress they have made, how they have been involved, whether they have been attentive and enjoyed it! If they've moved forward by the end of the lesson from where they started, then that's what we're looking for.

To get to this point, careful preparation and planning needs to have taken place behind the scenes. It doesn't happen very often that you can just roll up to school in the morning and deliver an outstanding lesson without some sort of prior planning! This is because you need to have a clear idea in your mind of what you want the children to have learned by the end of the lesson, and this is what you want them to reflect upon.

What this book will do is give you the tools you need to release the outstanding teacher lurking inside you. It won't necessarily be an easy ride (although it certainly won't be that difficult!), it definitely won't happen overnight and it certainly won't happen if you just pick a few activities from a couple of the chapters and use them in your classroom. This is an important point. Although the strategies in this book are *guaranteed* to work in the primary classroom, and although these strategies constitute outstanding practice, you can't just pluck them out of the book and use them and ... 'Hey presto; I'm outstanding!' Not quite!

## The outstanding philosophy

This, for me, is the essence of this book. You, as a practitioner, need to think as an outstanding teacher. You will need to think of every part of your lesson and think about how it can be made outstanding. You need, perhaps, to throw away some of the ways you've been doing things, maybe reintroduce something you've tried before in a different way, because there are certain things you have to do to make a lesson outstanding. And they may require a shift in your perception. Let's think about it another way. If you're already outstanding, fantastic! Very well done you! This book will help you to develop that practice, and give you some new ideas and ways of doing things. However, if you're not outstanding yet, there is a reason for that. And that is something you will have to face if you want to move on and improve. And that can be a tough thing to do. But it most certainly is possible! A few years ago I went on some FA football coaching courses to get my coaching qualifications. One thing that was said to us by an instructor was that you have to make change happen; you have to *want* to make it happen, before it will. He used the phrase: 'If you always do what you've always done, then you'll always get what you've always got.' How true is that statement? It works so well for us teachers too. If you aren't willing to look at and change your practice, then you'll never improve. And that's what this book is about. Each of the chapters in the book looks at a different aspect of the outstanding lesson and gives some strategies and ideas to help you reach that goal. Each of them has been tried and tested in the classroom and I can guarantee they all work! However – and here I go again on my soap box – they will only work effectively if the philosophy behind them is the correct one. 'I am trying this approach because by doing it the children in my class will be able to do _____ better and therefore their ability to learn will improve.' Not, 'This is a nice activity for a Friday afternoon, and it's from that Outstanding book so it must make my lesson better.'

You can read the whole book from cover to cover and try to get an overview of the whole 'outstanding' experience, or you can identify which areas you feel you would like to tackle first and jump straight into that chapter. Both approaches work equally well. Remember, though, the key to outstanding teaching and learning is in you, as the teacher, knowing where your children are (and no, 'In the classroom' isn't what we mean here) and where they need to go next. Just as important, they need to know it too. So spend some time on Chapters 5 (Assessment for Learning) and 4 (Personalized learning). Chapter 5 will give you plenty of advice and strategies to improve this oh-so-important area of outstanding classroom practice.

At the beginning of each chapter you will see this icon:

This will give you the background: the low-down on the chapter. What's it all about? Where's it come from? That kind of thing. It's important to read this section, as it will give you the context of the activities that follow. Talking of which...

Many of the chapters, after 'What's it all about?', are split into a number of sections:

By this time tomorrow

By this time next month

By this time next term

Each of these sections aims to give you an idea of how long it might take to introduce individual activities. This doesn't mean, however, that it will take you that long to get it working. Not at all. Something might be in the 'By this time next term' section for a number of reasons, as outlined below.

There may be some preparation of resources involved, so it gives you a bit longer to get them organized.

There may be a need for you to 'get your head round it' a bit more before introducing it.

It relies on you having done some preparatory work beforehand, maybe a different activity of a different type.

It may mean that it requires establishing in your classroom over a longer period of time before it makes an impact.

It may mean that children or TAs need additional time to get used to a new concept.

Please don't be put off by this, though; none of the activities in any section are difficult, nor overly time consuming. They are all designed to be used within the classroom to make a positive impact and I know, from bitter experience, that if something is too difficult, or too time-intensive, then it gets dumped right in the rubbish bin!

This book's aim is to make you an outstanding teacher – not occasionally, not just when you're being observed, but most, if not all, of the time. I say 'most' because we all have our off days, when it just won't happen no matter how hard we try! By developing some of these ideas though (and sticking with them), and by following the philosophy of trying to improve your practice, you will become a much better teacher. And that's what we're trying to do. If you're a better teacher, then your children will have a better learning experience and their progress will be better. It's a win-win situation really!

So, off you go. Choose your method of delving in and go for it! Use this book to help you become a better teacher – it's been written to be used again and again and not just read once and dumped on a shelf!

The journey begins here. Now go and become outstanding.

# 2 Outstanding … Relationships

Want the children in your class to think you are the most fantastic  teacher ever (and I don't just mean at Christmas or the end of the year when they deliver all those wonderful platitudes in a card and on a 'You're the Best Teacher Ever' mug – and then promptly forget all about you come the following September)? Or your fellow staff to all be banging on the Head's door every year just to get the chance to work with you? Want all the parents (or guardians) to want their child to be in your class? Forever?! Well, read on.

Relationships. Probably *the* most important aspect of not only outstanding teaching, or teaching in general, but life. Without good relationships with the children we teach, or the staff we work with (or the people we live with), everything can very quickly go pear-shaped. Never underestimate the power of great relationships – they can make things so much easier!

So, that's the easy bit out of the way then. But how do we get there? As teachers, we naturally form relationships with the children we teach, so we're off to a good start there. However, there are always going to be times when relationships don't work out quite as we'd like, and different groups of people can make life difficult: children (unintentionally), staff (sometimes unintentionally) and parents (who only ever want what they think is best for their child). So you need to accept that this may sometimes be the case, and then work with it. Easier said than done, you might think.

Let's look at what the eminent psychologist Dr Carl Rogers thought about developing and maintaining great relationships, and then use some simple ideas that you can implement.

Dr Rogers revolutionized psychotherapy in the 1950s with a client-centred therapeutic approach. He revolutionized the way people dealt with people. Dr Rogers said that in all relationships, personal or professional, there are three things we need to do:

- be congruent (genuine)
- be empathetic
- show respect.

If we use all of these in our relationships, then we would be treating others with 'unconditional positive regard'. Well, that's the basis of it anyway. Now, I'm not claiming to be a psychoanalytical genius (took me long enough to work out how to spell it), but it would appear that this looks very similar to the old Bible maxim of 'Do unto others as you would have them do unto you' – which is really quite simple when you think about it! I've put all the strategies here in the context of children in your class, but many of them are applicable (with a little changing) to your relationships with anyone. OK, here we go ...

### Congruency (genuineness)

In this context being congruent refers to being genuine; in other words being your real self and not attempting to be someone, or something, you're not! We can try, occasionally, and sometimes unintentionally, to impress by attempting to appear as we think the other person would like us to – but don't; just be yourself! Being honest and genuine will help those all-important relationships to build. Remember, your role is as a teacher not as a friend. Don't be over-familiar and say something that may cause you problems later on.

### Empathy

A typical dictionary definition for 'empathy' might read something like: *'The intellectual identification with, or vicarious experiencing of, the feelings, thoughts or attitudes of another person.'*

Wow. Toughie. How often can we honestly say that we try to put ourselves in the shoes of someone else? To step truly into their shoes, taking on their values, beliefs and experiences in order to understand their point of view? To understand why they acted the way they did? This is as difficult as it gets from a relationship point of view, but if we can try to empathize we stand a much better chance of forming a really fantastic relationship.

## Respect

Respect is, like many other things, subjective. In its simplest form, it is accepting that what someone else says or does is good, relative to your own beliefs, ideas or prejudices. In other words, acceptance.

## In context

While the three principles we've just looked at are great in theory, it can be difficult to show someone empathy and respect when they have balled you out for something you may have said or done! Obviously it is not always possible to follow these ideals all the time, but the people who form the greatest relationships with the greatest number of people, and who are generally liked by everyone, have these qualities in abundance. And they can be used with adults and children, albeit in slightly different ways.

In the following pages are some ideas, strategies and tips for forming those important great relationships with the children we teach. Children want their ideas, thoughts and feelings to be valued; you can provide that atmosphere where they can express these without fear of ridicule. Don't forget, though, that many of these techniques, if adapted, will work well with adults too. I realize that some of them are obvious and you may even think of them as being patronizing. This is not my intention at all. Many of you will be doing lots of these things already, but now and again we all need a little reminder!

The activities intended to be used to help build up relationships between you and your class, and between the class members themselves. Remember to use the information you gather from these activities at a later date: 'Good morning Dean; how did the wedding go this weekend?'; 'Hi Daniel; did you beat your granddad again at snooker?' This is important: show the children you value them and it will improve your classroom atmosphere dramatically. Join in with the activities as much as possible; it's fantastic from a child's point of view when Miss joins in and tells everyone a little about herself. They can see you're human too! Don't underestimate this joining-in lark – it is extremely powerful.

### Smile!

I know, I know ... it's obvious. But how often do we do it? It's amazing how effective a simple smile can be. Smiling doesn't come naturally to all of us, all of the time – so (occasionally) we need to make the effort to do it! Think how it makes you feel if, when you've had a hard day and you really don't want to do the teaching thing anymore, the Head comes into the room, gives you a huge smile, and tells you that they were really pleased with the way your class behaved in assembly – they were a credit to you. Makes you feel so much better doesn't it? And that's the effect you can have on everyone you meet. Try it: smile at the children you pass in the corridor tomorrow and watch how their faces light up! They will know that you've noticed them and that you value them as a person. And that relationship will begin to build. In no time at all, children across the school will be smiling at you and saying 'hello' when they see *you* in the corridor.

### PRM (positive role model)
Again, another obvious one. But so crucial. You are, for some of the children you teach, the most positive, consistent person in their life. They come to school, in some cases, for a break from what can be a depressing and destructive home life. Show them how you would like them to grow up; show them the kind of person you would like them to become. Remember what we mentioned earlier: 'Do unto others as you would have them do unto you.' By following the tips here, you will become that PRM! Children will respect you, will look up to you, and will want to be the kind of person you are.

### Welcome!
Every morning, as each child enters your room give them eye contact and welcome them by using their name. If you miss anyone, because you are drawn into conversation or otherwise distracted, use that child's name as soon after as possible. This powerful tip will let the children know that you are valuing them individually.

### Welcome ... and ask
As you speak to each child in the morning, ask them how their evening or weekend went. Try to remember any small details they may have told you (or make sure you ask them!) and mention these when you say hello. Always ensure you listen to their responses too. They will, again, know that you value what they say.

## Activities with the children

*Tell me a fact*

Call out a name of someone in your class. They must stand up and tell everyone a fact about themselves. For example:

'Good morning Mr Dunn, I really enjoy playing chess.'

Great way of killing a few minutes (not that you'd ever need to, obviously!) and of getting some snippets of the interests of the children in your class. Then feed this back to them at a later point – when you welcome them, for example. Ask about their interests.

*Introduce me!*

In this activity, a child you've chosen introduces themselves, gives a fact about themselves and then introduces someone else. For example:

'My name's Eric and I love collecting stamps. This is Gerry. What do you like doing Gerry?'

This can be varied so that each child can introduce a fact they know about someone else. As well as providing you with a different means of gathering information, this activity also helps to promote peer relationships and the idea, from their point of view, of showing an interest in someone else.

*Walkabout*

Here's another variation on 'Introduce me'. This more closely mimics a real-life situation. Join in yourself – the kids love it. Be prepared for a queue to meet you, though!

Children get up and walk around the room, introducing themselves to someone by means of a handshake. Then they tell the person something about themselves – for example, a favourite sport, hobby, food or television programme. Encourage the children to think of something the other person is unlikely to know. You'll be amazed at what you find out! Again, this information can then be used at a later time when you are talking to the children.

*Link letters*

Children have to say their name and then say something about themselves starting with the last letter of their name. For example:

'My name is Marc; I like chocolate.'

'Hi, I'm Paula and apples are my favourite fruit.'

This can be varied in a number of ways: last letter of their surname; they have to choose another child and tell a fact about them beginning with the last letter of that child's name (or their own, for another variation); change from last letter to first letter and so on.

### To err is human

Challenge children to be 'put on the spot' to see how many facts they can remember about others in the class, without saying the words 'err', 'erm', 'um' and so on. For example:

'George's favourite sport is tennis; Naomi's favourite food is spaghetti ... err ...'

Time how long they keep going until they say the dreaded word! That then becomes the 'record' in your class other children have to aim to beat. This encourages them to learn something about people they don't normally play with.

### Jumbled names

Write some names of children in your class on the whiteboard or on some paper tacked to the wall, but with the letters jumbled. For example:

Jtnoanho (Jonathon)

Point to each of the names in turn. When 'Jonathon' recognizes his name (he might need prompting!) he stands and tells you and the class something about himself. It may be a good idea to make a note of these things for future reference. You can, if you wish, follow this up at a later time, showing (once again) that you are interested in them and the children's lives outside of school.

### Joke of the day

As it says! Just choose one every day and share it; the cornier the better. Children love to think of their teacher as having a sense of humour!

### Guess who?

Give each child a piece of paper. On it they write a brief description of themselves, but don't include their name. For example:

'I have green eyes. I have long blonde hair. My favourite sport is golf. I like to play chess.'

Collect these papers up and give them a shuffle. Pass them out to the children randomly. In turn, they each read out what is written on the paper; the rest of the class try to guess who is being described.

### Link it!

Ask the children to sit in a circle on the floor. Then start the game:

'I am Mr Dunn and I like watching cricket.'

You then 'pass' it on to the child on your right (or left).

'This is Mr Dunn and he likes watching cricket. I am Marc and I like eating ice-cream.'

The children continue to 'pass' it round the circle.

'This is Mr Dunn, he likes watching cricket. This is Marc and he likes eating ice-cream. I am Lucy and I like playing rugby' ...

... and so on. Again, try to remember as many facts as you can about the children. They will love it when you show an interest at a later date.

### It means a lot to me

Give each child a piece of paper. Ask them to draw something on the paper that means a lot to them. If they are willing, ask them to explain their drawing and why it has a meaning for them. This activity probably works best later into the term once they know you better and trust you more.

### What would you do?

Give the children some real-life scenarios and encourage them to suggest sensible solutions – for example:

a child from your class is always being sent to the Head for getting into trouble; you want to help them

there is someone in your class who always seems to be on their own at break and lunch times; how could you help them to make friends?

You can do this activity in pairs or small groups with each child reporting back to the whole class afterwards.

### This belongs to me

This activity is another variation on 'show and tell'. However, make it clear to the children that they can only choose one item to bring to the classroom, and that it has to be something important to them. It's always a good idea to give them a few days' notice so they can have a really good think! It works very well if you bring in something, too, that means a lot to you. This lets the children know you are willing to share a bit of your life with them, showing them that it's a two-way street. Again, very powerful stuff. My teacher's human. Wow!

### Find a strength

This activity works best when you have half an hour to spare away from the classroom (yes, I know, you're a teacher and you don't have too many of those!). Sit down (perhaps with a glass of wine or a cup of tea) with a class list of your children. Against every name, put down a real strength of that child. It can be anything at all, doesn't have to be academic or even school-based; it can be something they are good at outside of school. Refer to your completed list often, reinforcing to the children that you know what they are good at and that you are proud of them for it. Really powerful this one, because it shows you value them as individuals, giving them recognition.

### Emotions ladder

A great way of strengthening those relationships with the children. Put up a 'ladder' as a display on a wall somewhere in your room. The ladder itself can be set up in different ways. Please go to my website listed at the end of the book for resources to use in the classroom. Each of the children then have a picture of themselves, or a card with their name on, and at different times during the day they, if they need to, put themselves somewhere on the ladder. This gives you an instant picture of who is feeling upset/depressed/angry/happy/ sad/ecstatic after break or lunchtime, and gives you the opportunity to address the issue straight away. It shows the children you care about their feelings.

### My flag

Give each child a flag outline; explain that each country has a flag and many have symbols, too; explain also that different parts of the flag depict something that is important to the country. Give some examples. Explain to the children that they are going to draw their own personal flag with symbols that represent themselves, or that mean something to them. Encourage them to discuss their flags with the class.

### My shield

Similar to 'My flag', except that children make their own shield, split into four sections. Each section contains a picture/symbol of something that is personal to them, or something they wish to achieve.

### Write the letter

Ask your children, either as a piece of homework or as part of their literacy lessons, to write a letter to themselves, detailing their thoughts on school, friends, family, etc. This task works well later in the year, when the class feel more comfortable with you as their teacher.

*Questionnaires*
These can be used throughout the year as an opportunity for children to express their thoughts, ideas and feelings. Keep them as open-ended as possible. As with all the tasks and activities, don't make it compulsory for children to share their answers.

*Plan it!*
Ask the children to draw a plan of their bedroom or their whole home. Ask them to take another child on a 'guided tour' of their home explaining, along the way, parts that are important to them and why.

*ID cards*
Give the children an outline of an identification card. The blank card should contain enough space for all the important information, e.g. name, age, hair colour, eye colour, favourite lesson, best friend, favourite food, etc.

## Parents

Occasionally, we may feel, let's face it, that some parents are only put on earth to make our daily lives miserable. It doesn't seem to matter what we say or do, they will always find something to moan to us about. Or that's how it can feel. In my experience, the better the relationships we can build with parents, the easier it makes things if there are any difficulties that arise later on.

Parents, as many of you may be, really only want what's best for their child(ren). I think we need to keep that in mind. On the whole, they really don't want to make a vendetta against you personally! So how can we help smooth the way to a better teacher–parent relationship? To be honest, it really is pretty simple. Well, the theory is anyway. Have a look at the following.

*Regular communication*
This could be through a home/school diary; a reading record; a homework diary; and/or a quick word on the playground. I've found that a whole-class email to parents who want it can be a fantastic way of letting them know what their children have been doing this week. Quick, easy and profitable! It doesn't need to be every day, or every week or even every half term. It just needs to be as regular as you feel would be of benefit. And keep it brief. Don't fall into the trap of only

getting in touch with the parents when there's a problem. They love to hear about something positive too! Do that, and you'll score loads of Brownie points.

### Be honest
Be honest but professional! Always. Always. Always. Even if it would be much easier to tell a little white one, don't be tempted. If you are known as a teacher who can be relied upon to be honest about their child, it will make your life easier in the long run.

### Be helpful
Be helpful/committed to helping their child(ren) to learn and develop. I know this sounds like it should go without saying – after all, it is our job! But always, if at all possible, find 5 minutes of your time for the parent who wants to ask how they could help their child(ren) at home.

### Be approachable
Have an open-door policy; be approachable. This doesn't mean parents can just walk into your classroom whenever they like. But make sure, if they ask to speak to you, that you find the time to do so. If you can't there and then, for whatever reason, always always always tell them you'll call them back to arrange a suitable time. And make sure you don't forget!

### Be professional
Always be professional. Parents will respect you for it.


## And so ...

As the teacher, it is important, if you really want the relationships with the children to blossom, to join in with these activities as often as you can. It may feel a little uncomfortable at first, but you will soon realize that the children love it. They'll welcome a little look into your life with open arms!

It's also worth noting that all these suggestions can be used with any adults within the school. Obviously you won't be playing the games with them (!), but the approaches themselves are the same.

And that's pretty much it! Easy eh?

# 3  Outstanding ... Planning

Planning. How much do you hate that word? How often, on a Sunday evening, have you sat looking at that blank piece of paper with the five week days staring back at you? How often have you just given up? We've all been there. The aim of this chapter is to get you thinking about your planning in a different way, to (hopefully) take away some of that pressure that is the weekly plan. We'll strip back planning to its bare minimum, to help you save lots of time in the process! I realize that all of you will have different planning forms and different expectations of your senior leadership team, but everything here should enhance, not detract from, your planning.

You will read elsewhere, and maybe have been told it by many people, that the more detailed your planning is the better your lessons will be; that you have to produce very detailed plans in order to achieve an outstanding lesson. Not true. At all. Your outstanding judgement is based on how well the children have learned, not how many words you have on your detailed lesson plan. I have seen lessons planned on the back of a cigarette packet (well, not literally you understand, but you get the idea) that have been outstanding; and I have seen lessons that have had planning equivalent to a Tolstoy epic that have barely been satisfactory. So don't get caught up with that assumption. It's quality, not quantity, that counts. It's how you deliver your lesson plan, and the outcomes, that are most important. However, there are certain things you can do, certain things you can include, that will convince anyone you know what you're talking about!

So, where to start? We'll have a look at the necessities for your plans first. Please note that although there'll be more of a focus on English and Maths planning (because those are the subjects that normally require more detail), most (if not all) of the things included can be used on planning for any subject.

Ok, let's get started.

## Planning basics

*Objectives*

The most important aspect of any plan is: what do you want the outcome of your lesson to be? What do you want the children in your class to have learned by the end of the lesson? This should be the first question you ask yourself. The reason you should sort this out right at the beginning is because this is what your outstanding lesson (or any lesson for that matter) should be about:

'What do I want the children in my class to have learned by the end of the lesson?'

I can't stress enough how important it is to do this FIRST. Remember, your outstanding lesson will only be outstanding if the outcomes of the lesson (the children's learning) are also outstanding. To be honest, nothing else matters. So this needs to be right. So, how do we do it then? Well, many teachers will fall into the trap of using an objective that describes the *activity* the children are doing, and not what they want them to actually learn. What do I mean by that? Here's an example:

LO (learning objective): to write a narrative story.

This is the *activity* the children are doing, not specifically what you want them to learn. Yes, you may well want the children to be able to write a fantastic story, but are you really expecting them to do that effectively after a lesson, or a week of lessons or even a fortnight of lessons? To write an effective story children need to be able to (in no particular order):

◆   use basic (and more complex) punctuation
◆   be able to use a range of sentence starters
◆   have a clear structure (e.g. beginning, middle, end)
◆   be able to develop characters and setting
◆   use a range of connectives
◆   use a range of interesting and challenging vocabulary …

The list goes on.

It's quite obvious that your children are not going to master that lot in a short space of time! However, you may want to focus on, for example, being able to use speech marks correctly. This would be your learning objective and you would, through writing a story, practise using speech marks correctly. It's important to be clear on this: your learning objective should be what you want your children to learn, not just describing the activity they're doing.

Here's another example.

LO: to be able to solve a problem.

OK, obviously this one comes up many times in Maths, but look at what's involved.

- Look for clues in the question (specific words; relevance to anything seen before; what do you need to find out?)
- Identify strategies.
- Try strategies, evaluating what you've done and checking whether the answer could be correct.
- Solve the problem using the correct strategy.
- Reflect on the answer. Does it seem correct? Does it answer the question? Is it close to your original estimate?

Again, as you can see, there is a lot involved. If you can do all of the above in one lesson then you certainly don't need this book. Or to ever to work again, for that matter, as you can sell your lesson around the world and retire on the millions you make.

So make that objective precise. It might take a while to get used to it, but persevere – because by getting this one right you're well on your way to knowing what specifically you want the children to learn. And if you know that, you can focus on how to get them there. Also, work out how to challenge them through the process – and then you have outstanding learning, and therefore an outstanding lesson. Good eh? There's more on objectives, and success criteria, in Chapter 5.

### Differentiation

Another extremely important link to make sure you have. Chapter 7 is all about differentiation, so all I will say here is that you need it. And you need it done properly. Because without it, you ain't getting outstanding!

### Support/Teaching Assistants

If you are lucky enough to have teaching assistants, make sure you plan for them. And make sure this is all shared with them too. Don't just put them with the lower ability all the time. See Chapter 13 where there is much more detailed advice on how to work effectively with Teaching Assistants.

### Assessment

Always show in your planning how, what and whom you are going to assess. Again, more on this in Chapter 5.

## IEPs/Specials Needs/G&T

You will need to show in your planning how you are catering for any children in your class who have Individual Education Plans (IEPs), those who have any other Special Needs, and children who have been identified as Gifted and Talented (G&T). This area will be covered in more detail in Chapter 7.

## Resources

Make a note of any specific resources you need: any particular texts, reference books, website addresses, etc. No need to list the obvious; if you need to write down pens, pencils and books then you might give out the wrong idea!

So these are the basics that need to be included on any plan. There are plenty of other things you can also include, as the following list shows.

## Questions

It's always a good idea to put some questions on your plan. You don't need to list every single question; you'll be looking at your plan all the time otherwise! It can be a good idea, however, to note some important questions to jog your memory. There's lots more on questioning in Chapter 8.

## Key information

This is important, especially if you are being observed. It's much, much better to have any information included on your plan; it saves the observer wondering or asking you stuff! So, what do we mean by 'key information'? Basically, it's anything that puts the lesson into context. For example, if you are doing an individual lesson plan (see later), you may want to note that this lesson is the third in a series of five focusing on developing the use of time connectives. Putting this in your plan gives the observer an idea where the children are coming from and where they are going to. Is it a lesson in which the children are doing little writing because you are working towards the oral telling of a story? Are they doing lots of writing as this is the culmination of a week's worth of planning? All this 'putting it into context' information ensures that anyone observing you can easily see what you are trying to achieve in light of what's gone before, or where you're aiming to go next. Also include any routines you have established; boy/girl numbers in the class; range of attainment levels; mixed ability or taught in sets (some primary schools set for Maths and English, I know) – in fact, anything you think will add extra information to help whoever is observing you ask fewer questions!

*Individual lesson plan*

Don't worry, I'm not suggesting for a moment that you do these all the time! However, these can be a good idea in preparation for being observed. They can put the whole of the lesson into a bigger context, and be more detailed so that the person observing you doesn't feel the need to ask so many questions! All of the above information is included, but more detail can be put into the 'key information' 'special needs' sections too. Observers will then have all the information they need so they won't bug you!

Planning sheets and conventions will be different for each of you, depending on your school and what is expected. Remember, though, that it's not about putting in as much detail as possible. You don't want to feel you have to keep looking at your plan to know what question to ask who next; this is a recipe for disaster that will put untold amounts of stress on you as well!

# 4 Outstanding ... Personalized Learning

Perhaps it is easier to start by saying what personalized learning is *not*. It made its first public appearance in a speech by (then prime minister) Tony Blair in 2003 and was, at that time, seen by him as part of the wider context of the personalization of public services. We're just going to look at it in the context of education (phew, I hear you mutter). So, what's it all about? It's *not* about you planning individual little lessons for every child. It's *not* about you letting all the children in your class 'learn what they want, when they want, or even if they want'. And it certainly *isn't* about making extra work for you, the already over-worked practitioner. It *is* about knowing what learning is required by every individual learner in your class, and making provision for that learning accordingly: moving the emphasis from quality *teaching* (which is still important) to quality *learning* for each individual child; a shift *away* from curriculum-led content at the centre, *towards* a more child-centred approach, producing a confident, competent learner.

Traditionally, education has been built around a fixed curriculum that is delivered to all the children, who are then tested at the end of the particular topic (or at the end of the year) to gauge what they can remember (or not). Personalized learning starts from the child, looking at what they can already do, building on that and supporting them to develop the skills needed in order for them to progress. Sounds difficult? Well, it's really not as complicated as you might think, and it needn't involve lots of extra work and planning either. Just a shift in perception from you, the teacher.

Many of the concepts around personalized learning have been around for years (for example, differentiation, covered in Chapter 7), while some are newer (for example, Assessment for Learning, covered in Chapter 5). Through its research, the Specialist Schools and Academies Trust (www.ssatrust.org.uk) has identified nine components to personalized learning. Don't worry, I've done the donkey work for you (after all, that's why you bought this book) and I've reduced that list to five. And, even better news, I'm going to focus on just two:

- ◆ effective teaching and learning
- ◆ Assessment for Learning.

(For those of you who are really interested, the other three are curriculum, organization of the school, and beyond the classroom. These fall outside of the scope of this book, as they are all related to whole-school issues rather than something you can make a big difference with in your own classroom. And let's face it, in the classroom is where it all happens.)

So, let's explain how the rest of this chapter works. It will focus on the first of the two points above – effective teaching and learning. We'll look at some activities and strategies you can use in the classroom to help with a personalized learning approach, and these can be easily fitted into your lessons. Because, in reality, much of the personalized learning approach is intertwined with assessment, many of the activities will give you the opportunity to make a quick assessment at the time. Even though some of these activities aren't in Chapter 5, they could have been! Remember, though, just using these activities won't make you an outstanding teacher; you have to include them as part of an overall philosophy for improvement. But I'm sure you're getting the picture on that now!

## Teaching

In order to personalize teaching as much as possible, you will need to address these key points.

- ◆ Create the best learning environment, allowing all children to take part and grow.
- ◆ Make sure the children are clear about you want them to learn, and that they have an understanding of the key vocabulary.
- ◆ Include *all* the children, making sure none of them are able to 'hide'.
- ◆ Review the learning as often as possible, including the child's voice as often as possible.

## Learning

By personalizing children's learning, you are opening the door to real progress. As with the teaching part, there are a number of points you will need to consider.

◆ Make sure all the children are clear about what is expected of them when the tasks or activities begin.
◆ Meet individual needs through differentiation.
◆ Ensure activities involve thinking in order to develop understanding.

The activities that follow will help you to address many of these points; the other points will be picked up in Chapters 5 and 7.

*Teach the cat*
This activity is listed first because, in my humble opinion, it's the one that has the potential to make a huge impact in the classroom. It certainly has in mine!

Many years ago, I went to a workshop about how to revise better for exams (I'd just failed one, so I thought it would be of some use!). I can't for the life of me remember the tutor's name (he was a retired professor and I think he may have been Polish), but I do remember that he carried out some research into the best ways to revise for exams. He found out that if you teach to someone else the stuff *you* want to learn, your recall rate dramatically increases, as does your understanding. Some bright spark also at this workshop said that he lived on his own, so didn't have anyone he could teach. He was asked if he had a pet, to which he replied he had a cat. So he was told to teach his cat. And that's how 'Teach the cat' was born.

Ask the children in your class to teach what they have learned to a partner or neighbour. It's not about *who* it's taught to; it's the process of talking through the concept. Make it specific and do it often during the day; in fact, do it as often as you can! You will see how powerful this technique is. Get each pair to teach the concept to each other, helping them both to remember something if they have forgotten a part of it. You can then get in a very quick, easy assessment opportunity by asking: 'Whose partner explained that [concept] well?' You can then progress this by having 'Teach the cat' experts who maybe wear 'Teach the cat' hats. These are children who understand the concept you are teaching and can share their knowledge with others in the class who haven't yet grasped it. (You will find that this group of children will change virtually every time, meaning each child in the class gets the opportunity to be the expert.)

This activity really does embed the learning in the child's mind and is a fantastic way of allowing the children to 'show off' what they know. It also provides you, the teacher, with a powerful, quick Assessment for Learning tool.

### Visual summary

There are a number of ways in which this idea can be used; the basic principle is the same for each. Start by making a summary of the learning to date (it might be just from today or it might be from a few days/weeks depending on the topic). This summary can be made on big pieces of paper, which are then tacked to the wall, or as a file to be used on your interactive whiteboard. (I would steer clear of using this on a normal write on/wipe off board, as you will eventually need to rub it off!) The summary can then be referred to, added to, discussed, questioned, etc. by you and by the children. Add pictures, notes, reminders and so on as you go through the topic/concept. You could use it like a timeline, introducing at the beginning what you are going to cover and when; this will give the children a big picture of where their learning is going over the coming weeks, along with the opportunity of adding to it or researching coming lessons at home. I would suggest the best way is to have it saved as a file on your computer that can then be projected onto your interactive whiteboard; when you've finished the topic, you can print off copies and give them to the children. They can then teach this to each other or take it home to teach to their parents. Lots of learning going on there!

### Hot seating

This activity is well-established now and many of you may already use it. A child (or the teacher, if you want to show them how it works) becomes the 'expert' on a given topic and sits in the hot seat. Questions are then asked by the rest of the class and answered in character by the person in the seat. This works well with characters or famous people you may have studied – for example, Roald Dahl, Queen Elizabeth I, Ghandi. It can also be used to good effect if you want to explore feelings in a certain situation – for example, a football referee who has made an important decision that causes controversy or someone who has caused damage to property by their actions. (Conflict scenarios like this work well when you hot seat both sides.)

*Grab 'em!*

Ever started to read a novel or watch a film and been engrossed form the word go? This is obviously deliberate on the author's or director's part to 'hook' you in. The same technique can be used to great effect in the classroom. Some of the best lessons start with the teacher leaving the children wanting more. For example, at the start of a Maths lesson, why not amaze your class with a mind-reading trick based on one of the four operations? If it's one you can easily teach the children afterwards, you're onto a winner! You'll have them interested instantly – attention grabbed! This makes it easier to gain their attention straight away – something that, as a teacher, makes your life much easier. There are lots more ideas in more detail, in Chapter 10.

*Press conference*

This activity fits in well with hot seating. Arrange children into small groups to take notes on a simulated press conference (or hot seating activity), which is presented by other children on a topic you're covering at the moment, or have already covered, or on any aspect of current or previous learning. The 'press pack' asks questions and takes notes. The activity can then be expanded into report writing, if required. This is a good way of children being able to share their learning, again being given the opportunity to explain what they know. The children taking the notes can also ask questions to 'bring out' more of the learning if they feel things have been missed.

*Tableau*

This idea works well whenever you are looking at a scene from a text or at a moment in history. Ask the children to arrange themselves as the scene, trying to convey what is happening at that point in time, and then freeze the scene. Other children walk around the tableau 'unfreezing' certain characters by tapping them on the shoulder and then asking them questions. Children in the tableau must remain 'in character'. This activity really helps the children to think as someone else, especially when the questioning happens. It forces them to think in a way they may not have otherwise experienced.

*Dictionary challenge*

Always have a pile of dictionaries on the children's desks. Whenever you come across a word in a text or on a website, or even that someone says, give the children 30 seconds (or longer depending on their ability) to find the word in the dictionary. Invite them to share their definition with the whole class. This competitive aspect is something children really enjoy and, again, it puts the learning back in their own hands rather than you, the teacher, telling them what a word means. This activity can then be used to 'teach the cat' to each other, explaining the word and what it means in that context.

### Bullet summary

Ask the children to prepare a bullet-point summary of their learning from the lesson. They can use this to present to the class or to teach what they have learned to each other. Again, this focuses the children on their own learning and enables them, and you, to identify any gaps in their knowledge and, consequently, the next steps required.

### Debrief

Have all the children sitting in a circle, as you would for a circle-time activity. Debrief the learning of the lesson using a range of open-ended questions. Here are some examples.

◆ What do you think you have learned from this lesson? Explain to a partner.
◆ How do we know that we have been successful?
◆ What could we make better next time?
◆ What have you learned that you'd like to share with the class?

This activity forces the children to think about their own learning, put it into context and verbalize that learning, thus embedding it.

## Using groups

 As teachers, we are told to use group work as often as possible, so the children can work with, and learn from, each other. Some teachers are very good at this; however, some are reluctant because of the difficulties it can throw up. Well-organized and tightly focused group work can be very effective, but if group work isn't set up correctly, with clear ground rules and precise organization, then you can easily find it doesn't go as planned! The activities that follow help to focus everyone in the group and ensure that group work is both worthwhile and beneficial.

### Record it

One of the most common problems when getting children to work in a small group – four in this case – is the chance that one person will do all the work and the other three will let them! When the teacher later praises the group for the work they've done, the person who did all the work can feel a little fed up! This activity helps to combat these issues.

Each group of four appoints a chairperson and a scribe. (Alternatively, you can make these appointments, if you feel it's easier.) The chair's role is to ensure that the task is completed in the time given; the scribe's role is to write down all the ideas put forward by the group and make a note of who said what. This is the important bit. You, as the teacher, will need to keep an eye on who, in which group, has made a contribution and praise them for it. The children will want you to notice them and what they have said, so will be eager to come up with ideas.

### The contract

This activity allows you to monitor more closely what each child in the group is doing. This works better with longer tasks – for example, if the group is researching a particular subject or topic. Ask the children to assign themselves a particular area to research and write this on a piece of paper. When all the children have an area to study, you sign their 'contract' saying that you agree with what they're doing and also letting them know that you'll be monitoring their progress. This allows them the freedom to work on their own, but also means they have to keep to the signed contract.

### Blockbusters

'Can I have a "P" please Bob?' Classic. That immortal line from a classic TV quiz show will fondly be remembered by many of a certain age. The idea of the quiz can be used in a multitude of subjects in the classroom. Children love playing it and because they are engaged, so they are likely to remember the definitions or teaching points more readily. If you're not sure how the quiz works, it's very simple. Players 'travel' across a board where each hexagon shape has a letter (or number) on it. If you get the correct answer (which begins with either the number or letter), the hexagon changes colour and you continue to the next hexagon shape. The idea is that you need to have a continuous coloured line from one side of the board to the other. The opposing team, in a different colour, has to try to do the same. There are plenty of free, downloadable templates on the internet (just Google Blockbusters game for kids); here's one that has lots of subjects all there ready to go: http://www.teachers-direct.co.uk/resources/quiz-busters/subjects/ks2.aspx.

For the game to be most effective, it needs to be a planned part of the lesson including some of the key words and vocabulary that you are currently using. For example, say the next letter is a C ...

What is the name of a word that is used to join two ideas, or sentences, together? (Answer: connective)

By doing this, you can introduce key vocabulary to the children in a way that is more likely to be remembered.

### Give us a clue

This activity helps children to focus on what they're reading and to pick out the facts, or even to 'read between the lines' for those higher-level inference and deduction skills. Ask the children to read a piece of text, find a part they understand, then write three clues about it that others in the class have to use to find the same information. You will be able to use this activity often, giving your pupils the opportunity to study texts closely in order to find clues for others; they will also have plenty of opportunity to study the same text using clues provided by others. This activity will allow the children to improve at reading texts closely and deciphering meaning.

### Fact or fib

This is a great activity that can be used in different ways and can also give you a very quick assessment opportunity. Each child is given a card with fact on one side and a fib on the other (please visit my website listed at the end of the book for resources for this activity). The activity can be used as a fun, quick way for understanding of the meaning of specific vocabulary, for example:

The word 'product', when used as a term in maths, means to subtract.

Children then hold up whether they think the statement is a 'fact' or a 'fib'.

The facts or fibs can also be used in a more open-ended way to elicit discussion, for example:

From reading this text, I think it's obvious that giving children homework is a very valuable and worthwhile idea.

This can produce some wonderful debates as, obviously, information can be interpreted differently by different people.

### Question time

If you want to review learning over a period of time, for example a term, then this activity is excellent.

Organise the children into small mixed-ability groups. One group is the 'experts' and it is their job to revise all they know on a given topic – give them around 15 minutes preparation time. The other group have to come up with a series of questions to ask the 'experts' on that topic, but they must know the answer themselves before they are allowed to ask them. Both groups benefit enormously from this activity; just be prepared for any debates that may ensue as a result!

*Pass it around*
This is one of my favourite activities, as it ensures that all the children in the class are focused all the time. You'll need two sets of numbered cards, each set numbered from 1 upwards depending how many children are in your class (you need one numbered card per pair of children – see resources website mentioned at the back of this book). Give each pair of children one of the numbered cards between them. Then ask all the children to think of a question based on whatever learning you want to check or revise. (Give them a couple of minutes to do this.) Then shuffle the other pack of numbered cards and choose a number. The number you choose, e.g. number 7, relates to the pair of children with that number. They then have to ask the question they have prepared. At this point, all the children in the class have to try and prepare an answer, because until you turn over the *next* card they have no idea who is going to be asked. Let's say you turn over number 2. The pair with that number attempt to answer the question asked by pair number 7. This can raise a lively debate and, once more, give you an opportunity for some quick Assessment of Learning.

It's incredible how this activity really focuses the children. They all have the chance of being asked, so consequently they all have to be attentive.

*Class plenary*
Choose a group of children for this activity. They get to lead the plenary session, led by a chosen Chairperson. Make sure they refer back to the objectives:

'Today we've been learning about equivalent fractions and we learnt that ...'

After they've explained what they've learnt, they can then choose another group to join in.

If you keep a note of these explanations on your interactive white-board they can be printed off at the end of the lesson and shared with the class. The strength of this activity is that the children are leading the review of the learning – therefore they're more interested! More personalisation!

### Display

In a fully personalized learning classroom, by the time children are in Key Stage 2, they should be taking responsibility for all the displays. They should be able to plan, design and produce the lettering for all the display areas in your room. OK, so I'm not suggesting you just hand over the reins completely and let them get on with it! However, by introducing a board that is theirs, the children can work on it to show off their learning. It can be used by different groups of children each term, ensuring all children have the opportunity to share their learning with the class. They absolutely love doing it; in fact they'll no doubt be begging you to let them do it all the time! By providing some focus for them initially, you can make sure it stays on track.

### Learning wall

This is similar idea to the previous idea, but not as structured. Choose a display space that can be used to stick on bits of paper, sticky notes, etc., that are relevant to a particular topic you are studying as a class. For example, children may be learning about the body in science. Quickly write down and stick on the board any vocabulary they mention or learn. Also write down any great answers the children give. Any pictures/diagrams the children make/bring in from home, stick on the board. You will find that this becomes a fantastic resource as the topic progresses and that the children will refer to it time and again.

### Concept maps

Concept maps, visual maps, idea maps, model maps are all different names for mind maps, brought to everyone's attention by Tony Buzan. (If you've never heard of him or used these maps, then visit http://www.thinkbuzan.com/uk/, or just Google mind maps.) The children love doing them, and they really are a fantastic way to personalize learning by giving the children a more focused way of preparing notes, plans, etc. and making each one completely personal to them. It's too much to cover in this book and you will need to teach the children how to use them properly, but it's well worth the effort.

### Learning logs

Learning logs are another brilliant way of personalizing learning. Each child has their own book, or log, where they make their own notes on their own learning. They can then take this home to share with (and teach) their parents/guardians. It keeps those all-important doors of communication open with parents and also helps to motivate the children by being able to share their work. They decide how they want to set it out, what they want to record, etc. It's not marked by the teacher; it's their own log. Danny Bullock, an AST in Leicester, has created a website (http://www.learninglogs.co.uk/) sharing lots of information about learning logs. He will happily answer any emails asking for advice.

All of the activities in this chapter have been used successfully in the classroom. Children love being able to personalize their learning, even if they don't realize they are doing it!

# 5 Outstanding ... Assessment for Learning

There are whole books about Assessment for Learning (AfL). Lots of them. Do a quick search on Amazon and you'll find more than 20 devoted to Assessment for Learning in schools. Crikey. No, I haven't read them all and, no, I'm not telling you to read them all either.

There have been big government initiatives around Assessment for Learning. I'm not going to go through this or even mention them really; this chapter is not going to focus on what tracking sheets, etc., you use to assess, but how you can make a quick, useful assessment that works in your classroom.

What I am going to do is give you, quickly and easily, the real nuts and bolts of AfL – the bits I know work. In its most basic form, AfL is: knowing what the children in your class know, what they don't know, and how you can make up the difference. This is at the heart of outstanding teaching. In this chapter you will be shown how you can ensure effective Assessment for Learning happens in your classroom – although it won't just magically start working. This is the one area where you need to devote time; no magic wands here I'm afraid!

There are ten guiding principles of AfL, developed by the Assessment Reform Group (www.assessment-reform-group.org). These are as follows.

1 AfL should be part of **effective planning** of teaching and learning.
2 AfL should focus on **how pupils learn**.
3 AfL should be **recognized as central to classroom practice**.
4 AfL should be regarded as **a key professional skill** for teachers.
5 AfL should be **sensitive and constructive** because any assessment has an emotional impact.
6 AfL should take account of the **importance of learners' motivation**.

7 AfL should **promote commitment to learning goals and a shared understanding of the criteria** by which they are assessed.
8 Learners should receive **constructive guidance about how to improve**.
9 AfL **develops learners' capacity for self-assessment** so that they can become reflective and self-managing.
10 AfL should **recognize the full range of achievement of all learners**.

These ten points make for quite a list! I'm not going to go through every one a point at a time, but just picking out some of the areas I think you really need to focus on.

If you want to make sure your teaching is consistently in the 'outstanding' category then you need to ensure that you make Assessment for Learning integral to your teaching and, as a result, your planning. You need to know where the children are so you can plan for where you need to take them next. Planning is of the utmost importance! If you're consistently including AfL in your planning then it becomes embedded in your classroom practice. Brownie points all round!

Make sure that your learning objectives are shared with the children. By being explicit about what you're looking for they will know whether they've achieved it or not! Always, always be clear in your expectations of them and how they'll know when they've done it.

One area that people get a little confused with is self-assessment. We do not expect children to be able to assess their own work and make the distinction between different level descriptors! That's your job as their teacher. You're not getting out of that one. It is perfectly plausible, however, for children to be able to assess their own learning, and to be able to verbalize what they think they have learned and what they think they need to improve. They need to be taught this and given time; it certainly isn't something that will be perfect from tomorrow morning! For example, 'Can you underline any embedded clauses in your work?'

This isn't just aimed at older children either. Children in Year 1, with some practice, can self-assess their own work to a pretty high degree, so don't just think 'Oh I work in Key Stage 1 and my children could never do that.' They can. Let them surprise you.

## Formative vs summative assessment

Before moving on, let's have a look at the difference between formative and summative assessment. I know many of you will know the difference, but for those who can never quite get the difference between the two, here's a quick explanation.

**Formative** assessment is what Assessment for Learning is; this kind of assessment in**FORM**s you on a day-to-day basis. The advice gained from this ongoing assessment will help learners know how to improve (and you to know how you can help them do it) through the small steps needed to make progress. It is short-term assessment.

**Summative** assessment is a **SUM**marizing of a child's achievement at the end of a time frame –for example, the level a child is working at at the end of a term or year. Most summative assessment is long-term and medium-term assessment. This data can then be used to report to parents, or to 'track' children's progress.

## The ideal learning environment for AfL

It is important to ensure that AfL becomes embedded in your classroom. But it will be difficult, if not impossible, to have any impact through the use of techniques mentioned here if the classroom environment is not right. I can give you all the techniques, all the component parts, all the key messages to embed AfL in you classroom, but ensuring the correct learning environment is achieved can't be done in the same way: the elements involved are less tangible. This will be discussed in detail in Chapter 6, but for now it would be useful to think of two main areas on which to focus:

◆ what children and teachers think of as being the best learning environment, and how to achieve it
◆ how teachers and children view each child's potential to learn, and how that links with the perceived ability of that child.

If these sound a bit tricky, don't worry! All will become clear. This chapter is set out slightly differently to others; some of the headings will have sub-headings of 'By this time tomorrow', 'By this time next month' and 'By this time next term', as in other chapters, and some of the headings won't. There is a very good reason for this in that not every area allows for this approach to work – for example, 'Objectives' deals with how to write objectives properly (as mentioned in Chapter 4). Therefore, there aren't some activities you can do straight away and different ones that may take you longer; an objective is an objective and you may get to grips with it quickly or it may take you a little longer.

## Objectives – effective ones!

This is the fundamental starting point for your lessons. Although I have seen lessons where the teacher explained to the class that the learning objectives would be 'discovered' during the lesson, and even a lesson where the children worked out the objectives during the plenary, I am suggesting that you start off with your learning objectives clearly displayed at the beginning of the lesson and that you refer to them during the lesson too. When you are comfortable with the whole AfL approach in your classroom, then it may be good to experiment with other ways of using objectives, but, for now, let's keep it simple!

Learning objectives and success criteria (SC; coming up later) are the fundamental tools that allow children to engage in their own learning. Remember what was discussed previously about the learning objective, and how it needs to relate to what you want the children to *learn* and not what *activity* you're asking them to do. In a bit more depth, you need to separate the objective from the context of the learning, making sure you focus the objective on the learning you want. For example:

'to be able to add 2-digit numbers using column addition'

is a good, focused learning objective. The activity the children do to achieve this may include using a calculator, or multilink cubes, or a 100 square, etc. Where it can become muddled is when you include the activity in the objective:

'to be able to add 2-digit numbers using column addition *on a calculator'*.

If you give the children a muddled learning objective it is easy for them to get more involved in what they are doing *rather than in what they should be learning*. It is an important distinction, and one that may take a while to get your head round! Don't worry if it's not completely clear straight away – just remember to focus that learning objective on what you want them to *learn*, not what they are *doing*.

*Open and closed learning objectives*
Learning objectives tend to be either *closed* or *open*. Closed learning objectives tend to be knowledge-based, are either right or wrong, and are achieved in the same way by all children. Some examples:

◆ to be able to end sentences with a full stop.
◆ to know the days of the week in Spanish
◆ to be able to add two 2-digit numbers together.

Open learning objectives, on the other hand, focus on skills which means there will be a difference in the outcome between children. Two children could both write a diary entry, including all the elements you would expect it to have, but there may be a vast difference in the quality of the writing. This second type of objective, obviously, gives you more scope to provide effective, developmental feedback, personalizing their learning even more. Some examples of open learning objectives:

◆ to be able to think of an effective simile
◆ to be able to write a description of a setting for a story.

The idea here is to make it clear to the children what the skill is that you want them to focus on. By doing this they are then more able to use this skill within other subjects. Here are some ideas of the different wording you can use depending on what you want the children to learn from the lesson:

◆ know that ... (knowledge)
◆ develop/be able to ... (skills)
◆ understand how/why ... (understanding)
◆ develop/be aware of ... (attributes and values)
◆ reflect on ... (metacognition)

## Success criteria

These, alongside focused learning objectives, are the building blocks for successful self- and peer-assessment (more on these later). Think of success criteria as steps towards achieving your learning objective. By giving these steps to the children, you are empowering them as learners, giving them the tools to recognize what they have done in their learning and what they need to do to improve. All sounds so simple, doesn't it?! It doesn't need to be too difficult though. Let's have a look at some success criteria for a closed learning objective first. With closed learning objectives, the success criteria nearly always have to be worked through in their entirety to achieve the required goal. All the steps normally have to be completed in the correct order. For example:

LO: to be able to use speech marks correctly.

Let's have a look at the success criteria we could have for this objective. Remember, we are looking to provide the children with the steps they need to climb in order to have achieved this objective. I would suggest around three success criteria for a closed objective. For example (I'll use 'Can I' statements, but you can word them to suit your style):

'Can I recognize speech marks in a text?'

'Can I put speech marks correctly around the spoken words?'

'Can I make sure the punctuation is in the correct place when using speech marks?'

I've put them here with the easiest at the top, but there's nothing to stop you putting the easiest one at the bottom of the list; this is just what's worked best for me. These can become teaching points during your input and, if displayed continuously throughout the lesson, can be valuable points of reference for the children.

Success criteria for open objectives work slightly differently. They can be compulsory, as with closed learning objectives, or they could be a list of things that need to be included, i.e. the criteria for writing instructions correctly. There are normally more than three of these, although I would suggest no more than five, and are used by the children as a 'checklist' of things to include. For example:

LO: to be able to write a persuasive argument.

And some success criteria:

'Have I included a paragraph explaining my viewpoint?'

'Have I given reasons for this, with evidence?'

'Have I included some alternative views?'

'Have I given an alternative course of action?'

'Have I written a conclusion?'

Once you have become comfortable with generating success criteria, the next step is pupils generating their own success criteria; it's also a great way of personalizing learning even more (remember I said there was lots of crossover). Success criteria have the maximum impact when they are generated by the children themselves.

*Remember:*
However your success criteria are generated, you need to make sure you refer back to them during, and at the end of, each lesson.

Here are some techniques for helping children to generate their own success criteria.

*Tell me!*
This activity works well with younger children, but can be used when introducing the concept of success criteria with older children for the first time. For example,

'Can you put these objects in order, starting with the smallest?'

When they obviously tell you that they can, make them give you the steps required to do it successfully.

*Do it wrong*
Demonstrate something to the children, but make sure you do it incorrectly. Let the children tell you what you are doing wrong, and what you should be doing instead! Write these steps down to help with the explanation of success criteria.

*Do it wrong again*
Show on the board a learning objective and a poorly written success criteria. Then proceed to follow the criteria and get something wrong (this works well in a Maths lesson). Encourage the children to discuss what has gone wrong, even though you followed the success criteria.

## Peer-assessment

It is easier for children to become confident at self-assessment when they are used to doing peer-assessment. Don't be scared by getting the children to assess themselves or each other; it's the next natural progression on the AfL road! You need to establish two clear ground rules before you begin.

◆ The purpose of self- and peer-assessment is to help children to have a better understanding of assessment and therefore what constitutes progress and success.

◆ Create a supportive, non-threatening environment where it is safe to share thoughts without the worry that any demoralizing, destructive comments will be allowed. It's important that children feel secure in this or you won't reap the maximum benefits.

Peer assessment will not be effective until you have discussed, shared and developed the correct use of learning objectives and success criteria. It may well be best, as you begin this, to use anonymous work from another class or, even better, a previous year. Keep the focus tight, ensuring that you don't ask the children to try to look at too much at once. The benefits of an anonymous approach are that the children learn all the skills necessary in order to make peer assessment work successfully without the stress that can come with trying to assess the work of other children from their class.

### The language of peer-assessment

Give the children, through posters on the wall if necessary, the correct language to use when peer-assessing. Some examples could include:

'This part works well, but you could ...'

'What made you use this [word/phrase/connective/simile/metaphor] and not another one?'

'I think that next time you ought to think about ...'

'I think you've achieved these two success criteria, but I'm not sure about the third. What do you think?'

And so on. Obviously, the kind of language used will be dependent on the age of the children.

There are many ways of using peer-assessment; I have included some approaches here.

### Three stars and a wish

Asking children to make judgements on others' work can be a little daunting for all involved. By using this technique you focus more on the positive. In a nutshell, the children give three things they think their partner has done well with (the stars), and one suggestion for improvement (the wish). Remember to keep those focuses specific!

### Feedback sandwich

Here is one way provide a feedback 'sandwich':

◆ positive comment
◆ *constructive criticism with an explanation how to improve*
◆ positive comment.

And here's a similar, but slightly different, way:

◆ contextual statement: '*I liked ... because ...*'
◆ '*Now/next time ...*'
◆ interactive statement (question): 'Why did you use ...'

### Plenary pals

This technique requires you to choose a pair (or small group) of children to take responsibility for the plenary at the end of your lesson. You will need to give them a few minutes before the plenary in order to get their thoughts together. If they feel confident enough they can discuss their work with the class and check it against the learning objective and success criteria. You could use a visualizer (if you have one; it's a type of camera that projects work straight from the book onto your interactive whiteboard), or have a piece of their work photocopied and handed round, or photocopied onto an overhead transparency and projected. Ensure they relate their learning back to the LO and SC.

### Swap it!

If you're feeling confident, this activity works very well; the children love it and it promotes healthy discussion. Give children the opportunity to assess your work or understanding of the concept being taught. Talk your way through your learning as if you were one of the children. Obviously make mistakes; the children will pick up on these and provide you with a good assessment opportunity – which children can both recognize that what you are doing or saying is wrong, and tell you how to improve or put right those mistakes.

### Peer smiley faces

Ask children to put a smiley face next to part of their partner's work that they like, and an unhappy face next to a part they think could be improved. Their partner has to try to work out why the face is there. This provides an opportunity to assess whether the child has a good understanding of the concept.

Peer-assessment of understanding, as well as work, can be very effective. The Question time activity from Chapter 4 is a good example of this. Ask children to set questions for each other to test understanding.

*Give me the answer*
Ask children, working in pairs, to provide an answer; their partner then tries to work out the question. For example:
'He had six wives.' *Answer: Henry VIII*

## Self-assessment

As soon as the children are confident with peer-assessment, they're ready to move on to self-assessment. The purpose of self-assessment is similar to that of peer-assessment:

♦ to recognize progress and success
♦ to identify how they can improve.

All the children should be aiming to improve on what they have done previously. We are back to what we talked about in the first paragraph, but with a slightly different slant:
'Where am I, as a learner; where do I need to go next; and how am I going to get there?'
By this stage, children are aware that they need a clear under-standing of what the learning objective and success criteria are. They understand that they need to monitor their progress alongside these. They have been exposed to regular peer-assessment activities and know that they are a natural part of learning, and not just an add-on that happens when someone is in the room watching their teacher! You will find that they are, by now, pretty good at looking at their own learning and evaluating it, and the step to self-assessment is a natural one.
Below are some activities and strategies than can be used to further enhance the AfL in your classroom. Again, all of these have been proven in a classroom setting and *do work*!

### Thumb-o-meter
Simple, quick, effective. Ask the children to show their under-standing of a concept by using their thumbs. Thumbs up means they understand; thumbs in the middle means not quite sure; thumbs down means they don't understand. So, what do you do with this information? Believe it or not, it's an incredibly powerful assessment tool and becomes even more so if you use that information straight away. Let me give you an example.

*It's just before the plenary; you gather the children together to elicit their understanding of the objective for the lesson. You use the Thumb-o-meter technique and find that four children have their thumbs down.*

Make a note of these four children (or ask your TA to). Then you can:

◆ spend the plenary giving them more input on the LO (the plenary itself can be run by the children, using the Plenary buddies activity earlier)

◆ send those four children outside the classroom (or to a quiet corner inside) with your TA (if you have one) to reinforce the LO

◆ make sure at some point before the end of the day you find 10 minutes to reinforce the learning with those four children

◆ make sure you work with them the next day on the same concept

◆ let a couple of confident children who do understand the learning work with those children for 10 minutes while you complete the plenary.

See how that can make a *huge* difference to the learning going on in your class? This is true AfL at work. Your children have identified a gap in their own learning and you have taken steps to remedy that gap straight away.

If you think the children are not being totally honest, or just looking to see what their friends are doing, then have them all close their eyes while they put their thumbs up. This also eases any embarrassment they may have.

Let's take this one step further. Do the Thumb-o-meter assessment activity just after you've completed your teacher input. Group the children in that lesson according to their own self-assessment. The pay-off from this can be fantastic: children who would normally always be in your lower ability group may, for certain concepts in certain lessons, have a better understanding, so consequently work in a different group with different children. All children feel they can work at a level that suits them. If they find that they have self-assessed incorrectly or that they grasp the concept better after a few minutes, they can move up or down a group accordingly. Imagine what that can do for their self-esteem, let alone their learning. This is Assessment for Learning working at its best to personalize the learning of the individual. Let them come in and observe that in action!

*Traffic lights*
This is a very simple activity that works roughly the same way as the Thumb-o-meter. It takes a little more preparation, but the results are similar. Each child has a set of traffic light cards; they hold up the one they think they are when asked to self-assess. Green means they understand; amber, or yellow, means not fully sure; red means don't understand yet. Again, quick, simple and easy.

*More traffic lights*
Extend the use of traffic lights by using them in this way.

♦ Have children put them out at the beginning of the lesson in front of them, face up. As you explain the learning objective and success criteria and continue through your input, the children can turn them over as their understanding increases. Note those that are still on red and do something about it!

♦ During individual work these cards can be turned over according to whether they need help or not. Green: I'm fine and can work independently; Amber: I can carry on working but need to ask something; Red: I'm stuck and I need some help. These can be picked up by others on the table and dealt with, without the need for you to be involved.

♦ When listening to others' explanations or presentations the cards can be used in this way: Green: I think I could have done better; Amber: about as well as I could have done; Red: better than I could have done.

♦ As a tool for pupils to assess their knowledge at the beginning and end of a topic and have clear ideas of where their gaps in knowledge are

♦ As a revision tool. Children can look at a topic's key words and traffic light them according to understanding. Homework could be to revise anything in red.

*Smiley face*
These work the same as the two smiley face activities earlier, but children use smiley faces to record their understanding. It can provide an opportunity for more detailed assessment, for example, a face with a furrowed brow – thinking very hard!

*Star ratings*
Another way of assessing their learning. Three stars means I understand; two means not fully; one means I don't understand yet.

*Bouncing!*

You can elicit understanding from children quite easily with this activity. You bounce answers around the room to build on children's understanding and help to right misconceptions. For example:

'Paul, what do you think of Sue's answer?'

'Sue, can you develop Carl's answer to include more detail?'

'Carl, how might we combine all we've heard into a single answer?'

*Exit poll*

Occasionally, it's a good idea to ask the children for an exit poll on the lesson, just before they go to break or lunch. Leave some scraps of paper and a ballot box by the door, and ask children to write down a comment about the lesson, for example:

♦ what they found useful
♦ what they found difficult
♦ an idea for a different way of teaching the lesson objective
♦ how the lesson could have been improved.

This focuses their thinking on the lesson just gone, and can give you, as the teacher, some real insight into their thinking.

*One-minute summary*

Give the children 1 minute towards the end of the lesson to write a summary of their learning, this gives you a good opportunity to check on understanding.

*Clear as mud*

As above, but give children 1 minute to write down anything they didn't understand. These can be collected by you at the end of the lesson to inform your next teaching. Real AfL at work!

## Self-evaluation

Self-evaluation is different from self-assessment. Self-evaluation is about learning *how* children learn. It involves an analysis of *how* they have learned and it involves skills that need to be planned and developed over time. We need to train children to self-evaluate – it doesn't just happen!

Here are some questions we can ask children after and about their learning.

◆ What really made you think? What did you find difficult?
◆ What do you need more help with?
◆ What are you pleased about?
◆ What have you learnt new this lesson?

Provide children with the time required to reflect on their learning; there are clear benefits to be gained.

◆ It increases self-esteem.
◆ Children recognize difficulties as a true sign of learning.
◆ They see that others have same problems.
◆ They develop an enthusiasm for reflection.

There are plenty of opportunities for self-evaluation; just make sure you fit them in!

## Marking

You are faced with enormous demands in terms of marking and assessment of children's work. Let's have a look at some back-of-the-cigarette-packet maths to illustrate the point.

You teach English and Maths every day.

You have 30 children in your class.

That's 60 books each night.

If you spend only 2 minutes per book, that's 2 hours every night; 10 hours per week. And that's without any other subject marking.

It doesn't need me to point out that 2 minutes per book is no time at all. It also doesn't need me to point out that this kind of marking load is unsustainable – especially when you look at what written feedback should aim to do, i.e.:

◆ enable the celebration of achievements in the work produced
◆ identify the next steps for learning
◆ provide information that will enable learners, and others, to monitor progress against standards and personal targets.

If we accept that these three points are important, then there is no way that we're going to do that in 2 minutes per book! So the whole marking thing comes crashing down around our ears. Therefore, we have to mark smarter. Obviously you have to follow your school's marking policy, but here are some ways to make your marking smarter.

### Rolling marking

You do not need to mark every single piece of work in detail. Keep a record and mark every third piece in detail. However, pupils are on a different marking cycle so you are marking after every lesson, but not every pupil's piece of work. Those who don't have detailed marking can work with others in peer-marking or assessment.

### Peer-marking

This is similar to peer-assessment in that children mark each other's work against a set of criteria. A 4:1 ratio works well here: four positive features against one feature for improvement.

### On the hunt

You provide the success criteria and the children, in pairs, hunt through their work to see if they can find evidence of them. Ensure they are actually looking for evidence of success, not evidence of failure.

### Detailed marking

When you are marking a piece of work in detail, use different types of written feedback:

'Can you please explain how ... why ...'

'I want you to ask yourself the following questions: If ...? Then ... why ... and how ...?'

'I was pleased with the way that you ...'

'I can see that you can ... Now I would like you to ...'

Remember that you want the children to be able to use your marking to develop their learning; by asking questions you can ensure that you do just that.

### Give time

*Always* give time in the next lesson for the children to respond to the written feedback you've given. This is a must for it to be truly effective. So, you've given all that great feedback to the children and you've allotted time in the next lesson for them to respond to it. In your feedback you've identified the next steps. The children then *feedforward*; this is the action of using the next steps you've given. This becomes their next step in learning and they can either respond to it straight away or make a note of it for next time.

And finally ...

### The best AfL resource ever

The humble, individual whiteboard. What a marvellous invention! Make sure every child in your class has one of these, along with a pen, for use *at all times*. Don't have any? Make some. A laminated piece of card works very well and is relatively cheap too. Use them regularly. They can be used for instant feedback from the children; they can hold them up and show you what they've done/what they've learned/what they're unsure of. They're great for allowing the children to practise, knowing they can rub it out if they're wrong. They're there for quick, instant writing when the children have an idea. Or when you have an idea that you want them to jot down. Instant assessment that can be left on the table for you to look at. And if the work done on them is fantastic, take a quick photo and put it up on the wall or into their books. As you can see, I like them. Well, love them would be closer to the truth. And you should too.

Undoubtedly Assessment for Learning should be at the heart of the teaching in every classroom. By following the steps here you will be well on your way to embedding AfL in your classroom and providing the children with the rich learning experience through which they can develop their potential.

# 6 Outstanding ... Classroom Management

Picture these two classrooms.

**Classroom A:** One phrase describes the look of this room at first glance – a complete mess. Displays are tatty (pupils' work isn't valued), resources are broken and strewn about the room. There are crisp packets and bits of paper on the floor. Equipment is stored haphazardly with no apparent order. Water isn't available. Closer inspection reveals the situation to be far worse. There are no routines. Chaos reigns!

**Classroom B:** The quality of the displays hits you as you walk through the door – awesome. A huge 3D cardboard model of a Tudor castle looms from one wall and is surrounded by carefully mounted examples of children's work. Other walls have a range of displays aimed at helping the children's learning. A variety of indoor plants creates a relaxing atmosphere and this is sometimes complimented by soft background music. Resources are tidily stored away in labelled areas. You can hear the laughter from the teacher and the children as they discuss the morning's lesson.

Which classroom would you prefer to work in?

Which classroom do you think the children would prefer to work in?

Which classroom do you think has the fewest behaviour problems? Each individual thing in classroom B is relatively insignificant. However, put them all together and they can make a huge difference to the atmosphere of that classroom. It is calm, organized and very likely to make the children feel that way too. They feel valued, they feel a sense of belonging, which in turn makes them feel happier about school. And a happy child is a child who is less likely to cause disruption.

In order to have an outstanding lesson (or any worthwhile lesson, for that matter) you need to have the optimum learning environment in your classroom – children wanting to learn and behaviour issues at a minimum. All of these strategies here have been tried and tested in the classroom (and I have the scars to prove it!) so you can be sure that, if followed, they will work for you too – making your classroom one that every child in the school wants to be a part of!

As you all know, children vary enormously in their levels of confidence, motivation, willingness to take part and behaviour. Our challenge is to provide a safe, caring, positive environment for learning to flourish, and this can be achieved through the use of clear, fair (they'll tell you if you're not!) and consistent systems in the classroom. And, believe it or not, this will work in any classroom, in any school. Yes there may need to be tweaks here and there, but by following these principles you will provide the children in your care with a place in which they can feel safe and valued, ensuring learning will happen! You may need to be patient with some of the strategies, however, as you may not see an instant change; but do keep on using them. I've used these techniques in a wide range of schools, with children of vastly different abilities and home backgrounds. And they work. So, let's have a look at how to obtain that great learning environment.

## Expectations

If I could choose one word to describe the best way to manage your classroom, the way to get the best from the children and the way to ensure they all make good progress, this word would be it: *expectations*. Ever watch any of those programmes where someone goes into people's houses to put right their unruly kids? You know the ones, where the children are running round like mad things, hitting out at anyone near and turning the air blue with their colourful use of language? By the end of every programme, every solution comes back to the same basic principle: high expectations. If you have high standards, and expect them, then the children will aspire to them too. This is pertinent to both behaviour management and learning.

Following your school's behaviour management policy, set your classroom rules with your class and 'start as you mean to go on'. This is important: set those expectations early and stick to them. I find it works well if you print these onto A3 paper and get the children to sign or even thumb print them to say that they agree with them. This then gives you something to refer back to if a situation occurs where any child is failing to follow one of the rules.

There are many different ways of managing disruptive behaviour and many good books on the subject (try *Getting the Buggers to Behave* by Sue Cowley). In this chapter I will give tips on dealing with disruptive behaviour along with some ideas and techniques to try to make your classroom a great place to be!

## The no. 1 secret for getting any child to behave

After years of working with children from all types of backgrounds, I've come to the conclusion that there is just one true key to unlock the secret of successful behaviour management. It doesn't matter how many effective teaching skills and useful behaviour strategies you have in your back pocket (although they can be very useful if used correctly) because without it, your efforts will eventually be in vain. The secret? The teacher–pupil relationship.

Don't underestimate this relationship. It is central to your success in behaviour management and if you do nothing but follow this advice (and try some of the techniques in Chapter 2), then your classroom will improve immeasurably.

## Alongside the no. 1 secret

Below are a few techniques and strategies for keeping disruptive behaviour to a minimum, for getting children's attention quickly and keeping it. They won't all work all of the time, so be sure to change/swap them around from time to time if you can see that their effectiveness is beginning to wear off, or if it's not working for a particular child.

### Voice volume

Try to vary the volume of your voice. This will ensure that the children have to keep on their toes to hear what you are saying, especially if you drop your voice. This can work better than raising your voice sometimes; if you feel the noise level is getting too high, instead of shouting over the top of the noise keep your volume lower. What you will find is that the children's noise will drop so they can hear you. This will probably start from the children closest to you and work its way back.

### Spell it out

Instead of just giving the children the instructions, spell them out a letter at a time. For example:

'T-A-K-E ... O-U-T ... Y-O-U-R ... M-A-T-H-S ... B-O-O-K-S.'

*Lip reading*
Challenge the children to 'read your lips' to try to work out what you
are saying. This is a good one for making sure that all the children are
looking at you and focusing on what you're doing.

*Moving in*
If you need to speak to a particular child concerning their behaviour,
don't shout at them from across the room. This could cause embarrassment from them, leading to them becoming confrontational.
Move towards them and speak quietly to them so the rest of the class
can't hear. Don't rush towards them though; this could, again, cause
a negative response from the child.

*Moving out*
Once you have spoken to the child it is very tempting to remain next
to them, waiting for them to comply. There is much more likelihood
of a successful outcome if you move away, *expecting* them to comply.
This enables the child to make the correct choice without the extra
stress of you being next to them.

*Attention getting*
There are loads of ways of getting children's attention. Here are a few
that work well.

◆ Ring a bell/tap a tambourine/hit some wind chimes. In fact,
   make a noise on anything that cuts through the noise! When the
   children hear it they stop what they're doing straight away and
   look at you.
◆ Have a 'special' word that you can call out. Make sure it's a word
   you're unlikely to use normally, for example, 'billabong'.
◆ Call and response. You call something, the children respond. This
   is their signal to stop what they're doing and listen to you. For
   example:
     ◆ You call: 'Ding Dong!' Response: 'Class announcement'
     ◆ This one from an old advert. You call: 'Skittles!' Response:
        'Taste the rainbow'
     ◆ With an army theme. You call: 'Attention!'Response: 'Ready
        Sir, yes Sir!' (or Miss, or your name, etc.)
     ◆ From the TV you call: 'Homer Simpson' Response: 'Doh!'
◆ All of these work well, and any new ones are only limited by
   imagination! Children absolutely love these and they work with
   any age (you'd be surprised how Year 6 love to make up their

own), but you will need to change them or have a big selection that you constantly rotate, as they can lose effectiveness.

♦ Clap a rhythm. Another call and response, but this time you clap a rhythm and the children copy it back to you.

Remember with all of these to praise the children who stop immediately; this will speed up the others too!

### Ask!

One of the best ways to find out about the ideal learning environment is to ask the children! You might be surprised at what they tell you. Try these questions.

♦ What do you want your classroom to be like?
♦ What do you want your teacher to be like?
♦ What helps you learn?
♦ What stops you from learning?

### Pairs

This activity helps to get children used to talking in pairs – perhaps with a partner they don't talk to very often. The results can be taken to a circle time-type activity for further discussion. Ask the children to walk around the room to the rhythm of a piece of music you're playing. When the music stops, they have to pair up with the nearest person and ask questions such as these.

♦ What is the best thing about learning in this classroom?
♦ What's your favourite lesson and why?
♦ What do you find distracts you most?

I've given a classroom slant to the questions, but they can be about anything at all –depending on the circumstances.

### Sign language

You can either learn some basic sign language (there are some great video clips at www.britishsignlanguage.com which may help) or make up some signals with your class. Instead of telling your pupils what you want them to do, just use your hands! As well as being fun, this will also keep their attention focused on you.

### Meet and greet

Some pupils are simply not ready to start learning first thing in the morning, normally due to factors outside of our control. Develop a routine with your TA (if you have one; otherwise a very sensible older child from another class tends to work well) to meet, greet and settle pupils down first thing. This can just be in the form of having a chat or working on an activity they really enjoy.

### Back in the USSR

The afternoons can be difficult for some children, especially after the excitement of lunchtime. An old and trusted method is USSR (Uninterrupted Sustained Silent Reading). Include yourself in this; let the children see that their teacher enjoys reading too. This helps by giving a calm, quiet atmosphere in your classroom and a routine that children can rely on. Vary it during the week with ...

### The good ol' USA ...

... Uninterrupted Silent Activity. This works especially well with children who struggle with reading. By allowing them, occasionally, to do an activity rather than just read, it takes off the pressure if their reading is poor.

### Reflection time

Allow, whenever possible, time for the children to reflect. This can be after part of a story you're reading or during the lessons themselves. It is always a good idea to plan in some reflection time so that you can ask the children to comment on what they have heard or learned.

### Procedures and routines

It is always a good idea to set these up at the beginning of term, but it is never too late to introduce them. Routines bring a sense of order to classrooms, particularly if it's a large class. There are many activities that are, at times, being carried out simultaneously so, consequently, routines can reduce stress and difficulties and improve the atmosphere in the classroom. There are several routines and many jobs you can get children to carry out for you. Remember to change these monitors around frequently so every child feels the responsibility of doing an important job. Some examples are:

- book monitors for giving out and collecting in
- Learning Objectives monitor who makes sure the objectives are ready for the next lesson

- ICT monitors who make sure the computers, etc., are switched on and ready
- resources monitor for things like scissors, individual white-boards, etc.
- Maths/English 'expert of the day'.

Routines also teach the behaviour we want to see in the children; it gives them the road to walk and a map to follow. And because this map is constantly repeated and doesn't change, it creates consistency for both teacher and pupil. Routines are the most effective, time-saving device any teacher can use.

Routines provide the link between the teacher's picture of good behaviour and the pupils' interpretation of that picture. They let the pupil know exactly what they have to do to succeed. For example, the end of a lesson is approaching and you want the children to tidy everything away as quickly as possible. So you give them one of these instructions:

1 'It's nearly time for lunch; put everything away and get ready for the bell.'
2 'It's lunchtime in 5 minutes; it's time to clear away. You know what to do.' (You then point to a clearly displayed routine on the wall which gives a bullet point list of what to do:

- Close your books and make a neat pile on your desk.
- Put all your equipment away tidily.
- Tidy your desk and sit waiting for me to let you go.
- After you are given permission to go, push your chair in and leave quietly.

Which of these two instructions will have the best outcome? It's obvious that the second one, once embedded, will work the best. The first is too vague; put everything away where? What does 'get ready' mean? You can bet it's not the same as what you mean! By being explicit with routines, and by introducing them one at a time, you make life much easier for all concerned. You could introduce timed music for them to tidy up to. Yes, these instructions will take time to practise and a week or two for each one to embed. And yes, you will have to give little reminders from time to time. But that's a small price to pay for a calm atmosphere in your classroom, with everyone knowing what is expected of them and when.

*Letting off steam*

Many of you will be familiar with Brain Gym® and how that works in the classroom. While I'm not a big fan of Brain Gym® I do think there's a place in the classroom for 'breaks'. By letting the children take part in a fun exercise or activity, it breaks that cycle of sitting, listening and writing. Get them up and have some fun! Any activity will do – some form of exercise, or aerobics, or even dance (they'll love it if you put some music on and let them loose!). All of these will help the children let off some steam and get them ready again for their learning.

*Listening time*

Make sure you don't have pupils sitting and listening for too long, either on the carpet or in their seats. Work on the rule of thumb of their age plus 2 minutes. So, for a Year 5 child, age 9 or 10, no longer than 12 minutes when they are just sitting and listening in one go. By doing this you will constantly be keeping them doing something, and the chances of classroom disruption will diminish. It's also worth mentioning listening rules at this point. You will need, in some cases, especially with younger children, to teach them good rules of listening. For example:

♦ eye contact with the person talking
♦ being able to sit still
♦ being able to sit quietly
♦ listening to everything that is said.

*Decisions and problems*

This is a fun activity that will help to build a togetherness that is so important to a harmonious classroom. Any problems or decisions can be given as a prompt for a group to work out together. For example: provide the group with a list of occupations – teacher, doctor, mechanic, policeman, builder, etc., then ask the children to list them in terms of importance, and why.

*Good listening cards*

This strategy works very well and encourages the children to give you their full attention. Have a pile of good listening cards available and give them out (or perhaps your TA can do this) to anyone showing you good listening during your teacher input or the plenary. For every card each child gets, they can put their name into a box (like a ballot box), from which you draw a name at the end of each week. That child then gets a reward. The more cards they get, the more times their name appears in the box, the more chance they have of winning.

## Seating

Experienced teachers will have experimented with many different table layouts in their classrooms. No single layout will be perfect for every situation, and no single layout will be perfect for all children. Sometimes the classroom itself, depending on its size, may well make the decision for you! Whatever you decide for your seating plan, remember to change the children round often, at least once every half-term. It's also a good idea to have different seats for different subjects, and mix these round often too. You could also have different seating arrangements for different types of group activity. By changing the seating often, children get used to working with other children and you reduce the chance of disruptions arising.

There are many ways of making your classroom a positive place in which to be. Using rewards is a popular way of encouraging children to behave in a manner you would like. Be careful, however, that the reward doesn't become the reason for the good behaviour; you need to make sure they are behaving because they *want* to rather than because you are giving them a prize! Making sure that you are fair, consistent and have high expectations of the children will ensure that this happens. As I've mentioned before (lots, by the looks of it!) many of the techniques in this book cannot be neatly pigeon-holed into one particular area. Some of the ideas and activities I've included in other chapters will have an impact on your classroom atmosphere, and can make your classroom a fantastic place in which to spend time!

# 7 Outstanding ... Differentiation

Alongside 'planning', 'differentiation' is the one word that many teachers shy away from if at all possible! It's no doubt down to the perceived difficulty with differentiation and the thought of how much extra time it takes up. None of these need be the case, however. Differentiation tends to be traditionally done by task (acceptable!), outcome (NO!), support (OK too) or resources. Whatever you may think differentiation is, there are plenty of things it is not. Don't get yourself bogged down in the thought that you have to individually personalise each lesson that you teach – a class of children each being delivered their own specific-to-them lesson. No piles of individualised photocopied worksheets either. Differentiation is wait for it ...

**Making each lesson as accessible as possible to every child in your class.**

Sounds easy when you put it like that doesn't it? And, believe it or not, it doesn't have to be difficult! There, I've said it. You can all rest easy now. Ah, but I can hear you whispering, *how*? Well, that's where this chapter comes in. As with every chapter in this book, the aim is to make the difficult things much easier. After all, that's what we all want isn't it? Let's get on with it then.

I've no doubt that you will be doing some differentiation already, which means many of the ideas that follow may not be new to you. You may find a different slant on them though, so please keep reading!

## Grouping

You can group children in various ways: by gender, by friendship, by similar ability, by mixed ability, by personality and just at random! You can use specific groups for some subjects, or for all subjects. You can keep the groups the same, or vary them according to subject or task. Make sure you are clear in your own mind how your groups are set up and for what reason.

*Things to think about*
♦   Why are the children grouped in a particular way?
♦   What advantages are there to grouping the children according to set criteria?
♦   Do the groups change, or do they always stay the same?
♦   Are the planned groups working effectively?
♦   How do you prepare for group work?
♦   How do you know if the groups are working effectively?
♦   Are the groups manageable?

It's important that you have a clear vision of you want the group to achieve and why you are setting groups up in a particular way. It's easy to get drawn into 'I'll have all my top ability children working on this table, and my middle ability working on these tables, and my lower ability working with this teaching assistant over here'. While this may sometimes work in some situations and for some subjects or activities, it is much better to change groupings on a regular basis. It will incentivize the children; it will enable children who don't normally work together to build a relationship; it can change the learning for many children by being able to talk things through with a child of a different ability. There are many benefits to regularly changing the groupings in your class and, as an added bonus, you will find that any behavioural issues will lessen the more you move the children around.
   Let's have a look at some grouping strategies.

*Collaborative group work*
Collaborative work is where a group of pupils (any more than two really!) work together on the discussion, planning and (if appropriate) writing of a piece of work. They work together on each of the areas, producing **one** piece of work at the end of the activity. This works well for all abilities of children, but especially well for children of a lower ability.

*Co-operative work*
This is very similar to collaborative work, where the children work together, but different in as much as the teacher will decide what the design, plan, etc., should be and directs the group more specifi-cally. Also, the teacher can expect one piece of work from each group

member based on their group findings rather than one piece of work from the group as a whole.

When group-working skills you need to think about:

◆ co-operation
◆ communication skills
◆ tolerance
◆ being able (and willing!) to compromise
◆ being able to take turns
◆ organization of tasks and time.

## Cascading
A group of children work on a task, or concept or any new learning and, once confident, share or 'cascade' that learning down to other children. This can work well for a more able or gifted and talented group.

## Paired teaching
This is similar to cascading, but in a one-to-one mode! Pair a more able child with a less able child in order to develop learning.

## Wheel within a wheel
Sit the children in two circles, one inside the other with the children facing each other. Children in the outer circle explain a concept or some of their learning to a child in the inner circle. Then swap over. The 'Teach the cat' activity (from Chapter 4) would work well here.

## Envoy
Different groups work on the same task, or parts of the same task. Then, when they have collected some information, one person (the 'envoy') reports that information to another group. This works well in ability groups where each group could be working on a part of a text (looking at different grammatical areas, for example), which then could be brought together. The beauty of this is that all children will be working on the same text, so it's not obvious which group is doing 'harder' work or which is the lower ability group.

## Goldfish
Similar to the envoy activity, except in this one each group is working on part of a sequence –for example, the different stages in a process in science – which they then pass on. The next group discusses how

that stage of the sequence fits in with what they were doing. Haven't got a clue why it's called goldfish (or am I missing something really obvious?).

### Snowball

A good activity for mixed-ability groups. See the detailed explanation in Chapter 8.

### Jigsaw

I love this activity. Great for differentiation and great for classroom management too! Bit of explaining, but bear with me – it's worth it!

The idea is that a small group of children work together to produce a finished product that is made up of different parts. Each member of the group has responsibility for one of those parts and when they're all put together you have the whole – hence the name jigsaw! Here's a worked example.

◆ Split your children into groups of five or six (let's assume we have a class of 24, so we'll have four groups of six).
◆ Decide on a task the whole group has to complete – for example, they're going to plan a party.
◆ **Task A:** to compose an invite.
◆ **Task B:** to work out a plan for the activities, working to a given time frame.
◆ **Task C:** to work out the cost of the food, from a given shopping menu.
◆ **Task D:** to write a letter to be sent along with the invite.

This is great for cross-curricular, too, especially if you have identified through your wonderful use of Assessment for Learning (see Chapter 5) that children have some gaps missing in English or Maths that you could fill here. OK, so let's say, for the sake of argument, that Tasks B and C are the most challenging, Task D is an average challenge and Task A is the least challenging. In each group, the children (or you) decide who does which task (and you will have some tasks being done by two children).

Here's where the differentiation comes in, and this really is ticking all the boxes! All the children doing Task A leave their original groups and get together to work on the task set. So do the children doing the other tasks. You now have all the children doing Task A together, all doing Task B together and so on. Every child has to do their own version of the task they have been given, but does so with the support of the other children doing the same task.

After a given length of time, everyone returns to their original group taking their part of the 'jigsaw' with them. And then the jigsaw is complete! Great activity, support on many levels, all children feel they have an equal responsibility and you get to focus on any areas of learning that need reinforcing with the children while showing great differentiation and personalized learning all at the same time. Phew!

### *Swap around pairs*

Children work in pairs on a specific task. On a given signal, one from each pair swaps with another child. Then they report to their new partner what they've been doing or what they've learned, or to add to their learning in some way.

### *Pupils as the teacher!*

This activity is great for giving children a real sense of achievement. It's something you will need to do over a few sessions. For the first time you do this, choose a topic that children have already done some work on. Each group should come up with a 'teaching pack' of activities and resources which they prepare to show to an invited audience – parents, for example. They then have to use their resource to 'teach' what they have learned.

### *Learning styles*

I'm sure we're all aware of the different learning styles and how learners are supposed to learn much better if learning through their own 'style'. To be honest, I've never found this strategy improves the learning by leaps and bounds, and I can't find any reliable research that says it does either. However, to provide a range of tasks through visual, auditory and kinaesthetic ways is of benefit. We all need to be exposed to different ways of using and learning new information, so make sure your lessons have a mixture of all of these; don't get bogged down into 'finding out' what each child's supposed preferred learning style is and making their activities fit that style. It just ain't worth it! And, besides that, it don't work!

### *Differentiation by questioning*

There are lots of ideas in Chapter 8, but I want to look here at something that fits in the differentiation bit quite well. It is possible for many lessons to differentiate by the question you give the children for their independent work. Instead of just giving different versions of the same worksheet (which, let's be honest, for a child is really boring), focus on giving each group an open-ended question. Let's say, for example, that your learning objective is to be able to use speech marks correctly in a sentence. Using some of the approaches explained in Chapter 8 could give us activity instructions looking like this.

**Group 1:** When do we use speech marks and what do they look like? Do we always follow this rule? Show me an example.

**Group 2** (give examples of right and wrong uses of speech marks): Why is one of these sentences grammatically correct and one not? Can you prepare a presentation explaining why for the end of the lesson?

**Group 3:** How can we change the placement of speech in a sentence to alter the dynamics of the story? Can you give an example?

While there is obvious differentiation here, all the groups have to be involved in thinking through their answers and providing reasons for how they got there. This is quick and easy to do and set up, but provides some real opportunities for deepening thinking and understanding.

*Differentiating extension*
You know what it's like: the activity you planned that was supposed to take all lesson has been completed by some bright spark in about three and a half minutes! And he's got it all right! So, what to do next? If you want to be outstanding, don't ever say 'Go and draw me a picture to go with it'! Here is a list of the type of thinking processes you can tap into to provide that extension:

◆ measure
◆ elaborate
◆ generalize
◆ describe
◆ restate
◆ gather evidence.

And here are some extra activities or questions you could have ready to follow these processes and give your early finishers something else to work towards. This can be adapted for any ability child too.

◆ Draw a diagram (*not* a picture!) to explain.
◆ Can you work on a demonstration of what you've learned to show the class in the plenary?

◆ Could you teach this concept to another child or adult? Plan how you would do that.
◆ Can you turn your findings into a graph?
◆ Can you plan how you would make a model of this?
◆ Is there a rule that you've found to explain this?
◆ Does this rule work for all examples?
◆ Which was the best strategy to use to work this out?

Many of these are useful in different subjects and some are more specific. As you can see, they are mostly questions, because questions are the way into that deeper understanding.

### More lesson differentiation
We have seen many different ways to differentiate lessons through the use of groups and through questioning. These are the two biggest, and easiest, methods to use. I can't stress enough how much extra progress can be made by all pupils if there is a bigger focus on questioning and group work, especially if the thinking is more open-ended. We need to encourage that higher-level thinking process more often, with all age groups.

### Plenary differentiation
By questioning, it is possible to ramp up those plenaries. The ideas in Chapter 11 will give you plenty to think about. However, remember that many of those ideas will hit the differentiation button too.

Remember, differentiation is making learning accessible to all children. Don't make the assumption that just because a child is working at a lower ability than others they are not capable of working on open-ended tasks and activities. It will be allowing them to work in this way that will open up the doors for their learning and ensure they can make the best progress possible. Likewise for the more able, they too ought to be given more freedom to explore, generalize, elaborate and debate.

So there you have it. Another brick in the wall of the outstanding lesson. More building coming up!

# 8 Outstanding ... Questioning

Most of us know how important quality questioning is, and its positive effect on learning. But how often do we do it? I remember back in my NQT year being observed by the Head who asked me how many questions I thought I'd asked during the first half-hour of the lesson (he'd been keeping a tally, the sly old fox!) I replied about 15. He then asked me how many I thought the children had asked, to which I replied about ten. Then he told me what the actual numbers were. Well, to say I was shocked was an understatement! I'd actually asked around 45(!) and the children had asked the grand total of three, and one of those was 'Can I go to the toilet please?'

Ironically, children are forever asking questions, especially when they're younger. How many of you, either parents or with experience of younger children, have been fed up with the constant 'Why?' question children are so fond of asking? How many times have you asked them to stop? (Or like my mum used to, reply with the answer 'Z'. Took me ages to work out why she said that.) Children ask higher order questions very early on, and we do our best much of the time to stamp it out of them!

Perhaps we don't always do what we know to be good practice, even though we may think we do. When thinking about my observation afterwards it got me wondering how good those questions actually were. If I'd averaged one and a half questions per minute, they couldn't have required too much in the way of deep thinking to come up with an answer! And so my quest began to make myself a better questioner. Some of this I'm going to share with you. Not all of it, because some of what I tried was a complete waste of time and effort – and the kids would probably tell you that too if they had the chance! But what I am going to share with you does work well and is tried and tested, so you can be sure it's worthwhile trying it for yourself.

Many questions that are asked in classrooms are *recall* types of questions, for example:

◆ What is seven squared?
◆ Can you remember something that we learned about photosynthesis last Science lesson?

These are *closed* questions in that they have a definite right or wrong answer. They are used as a way of jogging the children's memories or assessing what they know or can remember. But as a means of assessment, recall questions are next to useless unless they are asked of all children; one child's answer is clearly not reliable as a class indicator. These questions become more valid if the children are given a minute or two of paired talking before the answer is asked for, but even then they're not great. There are ways of using closed questioning to greater effect, and we'll look at those later.

I know many of you will have seen it before, but let's have a look at Bloom's Taxonomy. Bloom identified a hierarchy of questions that are very useful to the teacher. Table 1.1 shows it in action.

There are some great examples of the types of questions associated with Bloom's Taxonomy in the publication *Questions Worth Asking* from the Brighton and Hove LEA.

**Table 8.1 Bloom's Taxonomy**

| Hierarchy | What children need to do |
|---|---|
| Knowledge | recall, define, label, identify, match, name, describe, state |
| Comprehension | translate, predict, summarize, compare, describe, explain, classify |
| Application | solve, use, relate, demonstrate, interpret, apply, show |
| Analysis | analyse, infer, prioritize, reason, conclude, explain |
| Synthesis | design, create, reorganize, compose, reflect, hypothesize, summarize |
| Evaluation | evaluate, compare, contrast, judge, assess |

### Knowledge
+ *What is it called?*
+ *Where does ... come from?*
+ *When did it happen? Who?*
+ *What types of triangle are there?*

### Comprehension
+ *Why do they ...?*
+ *Explain what is happening in ...*
+ *So how is Tim feeling at this point?*
+ *What are the key features ...?*

### Application
+ *What do you think will happen next?*
+ *Why?*
+ *So which tool would be best for this?*
+ *Put the information into a graph.*
+ *Can you use what you now know to solve this problem?*

### Analysis
+ *What patterns can you see in the ways these verbs change?*
+ *Why did the Germans invade?*
+ *What assumptions are being made ...?*
+ *What is the function of ...?*

### Synthesis
+ *Compose a phrase of your own using a syncopated rhythm.*
+ *What is the writer's main point?*
+ *What ways could you test that theory?*
+ *What conclusions can you draw?*

### Evaluation
+ *Which slogan is likely to have the greatest impact?*
+ *Should they develop the greenfield or the brownfield site?*
+ *Which was the better strategy to use?*

It's a great idea to start looking at this hierarchy of questions and plan some of them into your lessons. By improving the questions we ask, we can show some pretty rapid improvement in the children's learning. So, the best way to go about it? Let's take it from the beginning.

*Wait time*

When you've asked a question it can be difficult to wait an appropriate time for an answer; but wait you must! The optimum wait time is around three seconds, which can seem like an eternity – especially if you're being observed! This amount of time gives the children an opportunity to think through their answers. It is better, however, if they are occasionally involved in something rather than just sitting there thinking. You can achieve this by doing one of the following.

◆ Allow children to chat to their talking partner for a given period of time.
◆ Allow children to jot down their thoughts on an individual whiteboard or scrap of paper.
◆ (You can still allow quiet thinking time; just remember to mix it up a little.)

If you give children extended thinking time you will find that you get a much better quality of answer and that more children are involved in the answer. I've found that children are also more able to challenge answers given and come up with alternative answers.

*No hands*

Be honest, how many of your lessons start with a recap of previous learning (maybe with closed questions) and have lots of eager hands shooting up into the air? And lots of hands that very rarely go up? And some that you have to direct questions to because their hands <u>never</u> go up? Even if you ask open, thought-provoking questions, do you rely on the hands up approach to getting answers? Lots of hands shooting up can interfere with the thinking process of some children (you will always get children who come up with an answer quicker than others), and it's possible that this happens so many times to some children that in the end they just give up and don't put their hands up ... or don't even bother to start thinking. And we all know where that downward spiral can lead. I'm not saying never use the hands up approach; it's great to see the enthusiasm of children when they know they have the answer and want to share it. But in order to have that all-inclusive classroom, with that outstanding learning for all, we need to mix things up a little.

So, how do we change it? Let's have a look at a few ways of avoiding this problem. Before asking, tell the children that it's a 'no hands up' question. This means you could ask *anyone* to answer, which raises the level of focus in the classroom. It can also raise the level of trepidation with the children too; what about if they don't know the answer? This is where your positive classroom environment helps out a great deal. Just keep reinforcing that it's OK not to know the answer. You do, however, expect them to reply to your question. A simple 'I don't know' will suffice or, better still, 'I'm not sure; I'd like someone else to help me out.' This means all the children are replying to your questions, even if they don't know the answer. Of course, you are going to get more 'I don't knows' if you continue to ask closed questions – you know it or you don't. By asking more open questions you will get a much better success rate with the answers given.

### Lollipop sticks

A great way of keeping children focused on your questioning, making differentiation better and easier for you and giving you a different way of choosing which child to ask is the use of lollipop sticks. Write each child's name on a lollipop stick and keep these in a container close to where you stand or sit to teach. When asking a question, randomly choose a lollipop stick from your container and that's the child who has to answer. Children love this approach, wondering who will come out next!

To take this one step further, and to really impress, use coloured lollipop sticks. These are available very cheaply in large packs (even to keep you going for years!) from educational suppliers. By using colours, you can differentiate your questioning. For example, have all your higher ability children in pink, middle ability in blue and lower ability in purple (swap colours regularly so children don't work it out and get upset). You can then either ask the question and choose which group would be most suited to answer, or choose a colour first and tailor your question to suit. That's fantastic, on-the-spot differentiation, even better if you tie it in with one of the self-assessment activities mentioned in Chapter 5. Some serious, specific, targeted learning going on now!

### Paired talking/talking partners

We mentioned these earlier. Talking partners are a great way of getting children talking about their learning. In Chapter 5, the Teach the cat activity uses paired talking, which is something that works fantastically well but that needs to be planned and, to some degree, taught. I will use both of the terms 'talking partner' and 'paired talking'. Essentially, they are the same thing, so don't be confused!

When you ask a question, allow 30 seconds or so for children to discuss the answer with their talking partner. I find it works very well to time this 30 seconds, perhaps by use of an egg timer, a short burst of music or one of the many timers available on the internet and projected on your interactive whiteboard. Here are a couple:

http://eggtimer.com/

http://www.online-stopwatch.com/full-screen-stopwatch/.

The answers can then be collected (no hands up) from a few pairs. Remember, all the time you are doing this you are giving the children more responsibility for their own learning, and this is what you need to be focusing on in order to become outstanding.

I would suggest using talking partners all the time in your class. It will enable each pupil to have a voice, become more confident in their role in the classroom and raise their self-esteem. You will need to do some management of this idea though.

♦ When you begin, and also as a reminder after a while, it is a good idea to model paired talking with another adult. It works well if you first model how *not* to do it. Some good ideas for successful talking partners are listed later.

♦ Change talking partners regularly. Use the lollipop sticks to randomly pull out children's names to sit together for about a three-week period. This will mean that children are working with other children they may not normally have anything to do with, which will impact on the positive nature in your classroom.

♦ Check each time you use paired talking that everyone has a partner. If not quickly move someone around, or just use threes instead.

Here are some skills you will need to share with your children in order for them to become good at paired talking,

♦ Look at your partner when you are talking to them.
♦ Don't let anything else going on around distract you.
♦ Think about what your partner is saying.
♦ Look interested.
♦ Listen carefully to your partner's point of view.
♦ Try to say more than a couple of words!
♦ Be prepared to compromise if necessary.

## Effective questioning

In her book *Active Learning Through Formative Assessment*, Shirley Clarke gives a list of five templates to use for asking effective questions. These are fantastic and work extremely well in the classroom; they personalize the learning more for the children and facilitate lots of discussion. They are based on basic recall questions, the type we most often ask, but really do change the way they are presented so a wider range of thinking and discussion can take place. We're going to have a look at how they work here.

### Getting the question right

Probably the hardest part of questioning is actually thinking up really effective questions – questions that will really challenge the children's thinking, causing them to deepen their understanding. This is where these five templates come in very useful indeed. Just be aware that children will need to have a basic understanding of the topic area first.

### Giving a range of answers

When giving the question, give a range of answers too. However, you're not just looking for the children to choose the correct answer. Using this strategy means that children have to decide which answers are correct, which are close answers (and why), which answers can't be right but there is a reason as to how they could have been arrived at, or which answers can't be right and, again, why. Here's an example.

**Question:** What makes a good friend?

**Range of answers given:** kindness, always honest, shares their sweets, a bully, someone good looking, someone loyal.

The answers consist of:

◆ two that are *definitely* right
◆ two that are clearly *wrong*
◆ two that promote discussion – sort of *it depends* answers.

This way of framing questions leads to much discussion.

### A statement

This strategy takes a recall question and turns it into a statement for children to discuss with their partner. It encourages debate and discussion and helps to develop critical thinking. Here's an example.

**Question:** Why did Goldilocks go into the three bears' cottage?

**Turned into a statement for discussion:** Goldilocks was a burglar. Do you agree or disagree, and why?

*Finding opposites*

This question-framing technique chooses a basic recall question and requires you to think of two examples: one of which is right, and one of which is wrong. Children have to decide which one is correct, which one isn't, and, more importantly, why. This type of question framing works well in maths and with grammar and spelling examples. It encourages problem solving, stimulates interest and makes the children give explanations.

**Question:** What do plants need to grow?

**And reframed** *(show two pictures or examples of a plant): Why is this plant healthy and this plant dying?*

*Giving the answer first*

Give the children the answer straight away and ask them to explain it. This strategy is a good one because it changes the emphasis a little from the answer itself, to discussing reasons for the answer. This one is also inclusive as all children can come with an idea or a reason at many different levels.

**Question:** Can you give me an example of a complex sentence?

**Reframed with the answer first:** This is a complex sentence. Why?

*An opposing standpoint*

This activity can be used for discussing controversial and sometimes sensitive subjects. It works well within PSHE (Personal Health and Social Education). Obviously, care needs to be taken if there is a sensitive issue. The question is taken from an opposing point of view, to provide real challenge for the children (and sometimes teachers!). These can be used in all situations though, not just controversial ones! Notice that these questions are good ones to begin with; often we're just trying to push even further. It improves persuasive and debating skills, develops respect for other people's point of view and can encourage thinking outside the box.

**Question:** Why is it wrong to steal?

**Opposing view:** What would a mother whose children were starving think about shoplifting?

*Socratic questioning*

Socrates is the father of Western philosophy (I'm sure you know). But did you realize he was also most probably the earliest champion of Assessment for Learning?! He was a firm believer in *ex duco*, which means drawing out or leading out from the student. (It's where our word 'education has' its root.) So, let's have a look at his questioning strategy. His main aim was to challenge statements in a way that moves the learner towards a deeper understanding. Just what we're looking for! This is achieved by moving through different stages of questioning, with each stage questioning a different facet of understanding. It's extended further through the search for proof and reasoning. Let's have a look at what this all means.

### Conceptual clarification questions

This gets the children to think more about what they are asking or thinking about, to prove the concepts behind their argument. Basic 'tell me more ' questions, such as those that follow, will bring out explanations.

- *Can you explain that?*
- *Can you explain what that means?*
- *Have we looked at this before?*
- *Can you give me an example?*
- *Re-word that for me, can you?*

### Probing assumptions

Probing of assumptions makes children think about the assumptions and beliefs on which of their argument rests. This is about getting them to provide evidence for their thinking.

- *What else could we assume?*
- *Why do you think that?*
- *How do we know that?*
- *Please explain why/how ...?*
- *What are your reasons?*
- *Do you agree or disagree with ...?*

### Questioning viewpoints and perspectives

Most arguments are given from a particular position. Here, you are looking for an alternative viewpoint.

- *Can you put it another way?*
- *What is the difference between ... and ...?*
- *Why is it better than ...?*
- *How are ... and ... similar?*

### Probe implications and consequences

This asks whether their thinking can form a general rule that can be applied elsewhere. More probing questions!

◆ *Then what would happen?*
◆ *What are the consequences of that assumption?*
◆ *How does it affect ... ?*
◆ *Does it agree with what we said before?*
◆ *Why is ... important?*
◆ *Is there a general rule for that?*

### Questions about the question

You can also get reflexive about the whole thing, turning the question in on itself. Very high-level thinking going on now.

◆ *What was the point of asking that question?*
◆ *Why do you think I asked this question?*
◆ *What does that mean?*
◆ *Are we any closer to answering the question/solving the problem?*

Obviously, much of this goes further than we would go in the primary classroom, but there are parts of it that can be used effectively to deepen children's thinking. All of these questioning strategies can be used in the classroom, with a little tweaking.

So, we've looked at lots of different questioning styles and activities guaranteed to up the level of discussion and deepen the thinking and understanding in your classroom. And really begin to personalize that learning.

Below are a few more ways of using questioning, in no particular order or preference! I can say, however, that they all work in the classroom!

### Conscience alley

This is a good way of eliciting understanding and questioning from the children when you've discussed a text and looked at characters,. Have the children form two rows opposite each other, with enough room for someone to walk down the middle. Then, similar to hot seating (see Chapter 4), choose a child to be the character you've been studying. Ask the child to walk slowly through the 'alley', stopping whenever someone asks a question. This is good for developing opinions and discussion of characters.

*Flashbacks and flash forwards*
Children focus on questions based on the consequences of action rather than on the action itself, as these examples show.

◆ 'What would have happened if Harry had chosen the other road to take?'
◆ 'Do you think it would have been easier if Molly had said "No"?'

*Snowball*
A great little activity for encouraging questioning. There are three parts to consider:

**Part 1:** Working independently, each child writes down one question asked for by the teacher. I'd give around 30 seconds to do this.
**Part 2:** Pair the children up (doesn't matter if mixed ability or other pairing) and their challenge is to find four questions between them.
**Part 3:** Put the children into groups of four. Now they need twelve questions. Best to give a couple of minutes for this.

When this process is complete, ask each group in turn to report back just one idea: their best. When questioning, it could work like this.

**Part 1:** 'Write down one question you would like to ask about anything to do with the text we've just looked at.'
**Part 2:** 'In pairs, see if you can find four interesting questions to ask about the text.'
**Part 3:** 'In your group, combine all your questions and see if there are any more. Now, this group over here, ask the question you think is the most interesting, or the question about the one thing that really is puzzling you.'

Again what you're doing here is tailoring the learning to fit in with the children's curiosity. You can still plan to reach similar conclusions to what you wanted to reach, but this method involves them more and repeatedly brings up things you had never even thought of.

*Exchange questioning*
In this activity, both the children and you prepare some questions on a given topic. You then chair a discussion around the questions inviting debate and higher-order questioning based on Bloom's Taxonomy (see Table 8.1 earlier in this chapter). This really can get quite intense!

*No hands up except ...*

... when you are commenting on another child's answer. Use this strategy when you are doing 'no hands up' questioning. Only allow hands up if someone has a question or comment to make about the answer given by another child. This invites deeper thinking about answers given, and, again, generates healthy debate.

Have a go at some of these activities; the children will really enjoy the difference and you will find that they begin to develop a much deeper understanding of many concepts.

# 9    Outstanding ...
       Community Cohesion

Community cohesion is a relatively new initiative for primary schools.
That said, it is definitely something we should all be aware of, even if
the specific activities we can do to promote it in our own classrooms
aren't as varied as in other areas of the curriculum. So what do we
mean by the term 'community cohesion'? It can probably be defined,
in its basic sense, as the promotion of positive relationships between
faith communities, ethnic groups, people of all (or no) disability,
people from different geographical areas and of different age, gender
and sexual orientation. In other words, everyone is working together
to promote a society in which everyone is equal and has the same
chances in life.

Since September 2007 all schools have had a duty to promote
community cohesion, and OFSTED has taken up the mantle of
inspecting how it is being addressed in schools since September 2008.
Our job in the classroom is to promote these ideals in the best way
that we can, encouraging everyone to contribute to this vision for the
area in which our school is situated while, at the same time, being
aware of similarities and differences within a wider context. We have
a crucial role in creating opportunities for all children to achieve their
potential and by developing them as thinking, tolerant adults.

## What is my school community?

The term 'community' has a number of meanings for schools. These
include the school community, the area (community) where the
school is located, and the wider United Kingdom and global communities. As a school the idea is to make sure your children have an
understanding of each of these and how they relate to them.

## Considerations for primary schools

Obviously these will vary greatly from school to school depending on the make-up of the school's population and the local community in which it is situated. Because of these differences, community cohesion will look different in different schools in different parts of the country – thus meaning there is no 'ideal' model. What we *can* do, however, is provide our children with as many opportunities as possible to be aware of who they are, how they are similar or different to others, and how everyone needs to work together to make their community a healthy one.

## Ideas for the classroom

♦ Use ideas like circle time, peer support, etc., to discuss community issues that you may be aware of or to discuss communities different from your own.

♦ Agree as a class that, wherever possible, you will fight bullying and racial stereotyping. Discuss these issues so that children are aware of them. Encourage open debate.

♦ Promote positive relationships with *everyone* regardless of race, religion, etc.

♦ Google earth. This is a great resource for showing children where their school is, and relating that to how tiny it is compared to the rest of the area/country/world. This can then be made into a display.

♦ In Maths, when working on data you can do an analysis of your local area in terms of shops, community areas, etc. This is a good way of determining how representative your school is of the community in which it resides.

♦ Set up a project based on a community, either local or further afield.

♦ Set up a class community newsletter that you can send out to the local community every half term detailing the kinds of things you've been up to and what you'd be interested in learning next. You may get some local people willing to come in to discuss things.

♦ Run a 'Window on the world' news activity. Each day, invite different children to find and report on a news story. It can be a story that is from the local community or something much further afield. Try to encourage pupils to look for stories that are different and tell a tale of a community. You could encourage them to establish a display in the classroom and take ownership of it.

◆ Celebrate other world festivals in your class (if they are not already celebrated in school) – for example, Chinese New Year, Diwali, etc.

◆ Set up a community badge scheme in your class as an award for children who either come up with the best idea for making a difference in the community or for a child who has done something in the community that's worthy of mention. This will raise the profile of the community in your school.

◆ Focus on a different job/area of work every week. Look in detail at what that job/employment entails and how it makes a difference in the community. The children could take ownership of this, perhaps turning it into a display area in the classroom or a corridor for other children to see.

◆ Invite people from the community – for example, local community and religious leaders, local business people, police and fire services, etc. – to come to the school and talk to your children, This will give the children a real idea of the people who live and work in their community every day.

◆ Try to set up a link with another school that is different in terms of its socio-economic or ethnic mix.

◆ Organize debates around local issues. (You could try to arrange to hold them in local council chambers at the local council town hall.)

◆ Have focus days that concentrate specifically on mixing age ranges and abilities. This is something you will have to organize as a school. It's a great activity for breaking down barriers between children who wouldn't normally have the opportunity to work together.

◆ Invite people of different religions into your school assembly to talk to the children about their faith and how it has many similarities to their own.

◆ Organize 'A day in the life of ...'. (NB This may need whole-school support.) A child is chosen to spend a day in the life of someone in their school community – for example, the Head, the school site manager, a dinner lady, etc. – in order to gain an idea of the jobs that people do around the school on a day-to-day basis. It could be run like an election where everyone has to vote on who they think would be best suited to the job; alternatively, it could be done as a competition prize or even just pull the name from a hat! That child would then have to report their findings to the rest of the class.

♦ Most schools have a school council or a student voice of some description. Encourage your pupils to perhaps adopt a charity for a year, where you can take part in different fundraising events to help deliver the message about people less fortunate than themselves.

♦ If your school doesn't have an eco team, which tries to improve the environment of the school and promote cleaner living and sustainability of resources, perhaps it is something that you could help to set up.

♦ You may have someone at your school who has had forest school training, or you may be aware of what it's all about. As part of the forest school ethos, children are taught about the environment in and around their school; it is a great way of helping them to understand about looking after the area they live in.

♦ Playground pals/buddies/friendship stops all take into account children who, for whatever reason, at playtime and lunchtime for don't have anyone to play with. By setting one or more of these ideas up, you are encouraging other children to be aware of people around them and how their actions can have an effect.

The area of community cohesion is a difficult one to specify activities for *just* in your classroom. Many of the ideas you have will need to be considered as a whole school – for example, a Christmas fayre inviting the local community, whole-school focus days, etc. However, this doesn't mean that you can't involve your children in being aware of different cultures, religions and people from different social backgrounds. You will be able to cover many of the issues in PSHE or circle time activities and Religious Education lessons. What is important is that you make children aware of these differences and similarities. Don't try to 'force' community cohesion into your lesson just because you are being observed; if you can fit an activity in, or even just mention something if it crops up during the lesson, then great. Otherwise, don't worry.

# 10 Outstanding ... Starters

The lesson starter, in many cases, can be the make or break of your lesson. No, I'm not trying to scare you witless, but if the starter isn't good enough that can set the tone for the whole lesson. Not just for the children sitting there with their expectant little faces, but also for any observer who may be sitting there with their expectant little faces too. A starter sets the tone. It gives that all-important first impression. It tells the children either: 'Yes! I'm really looking forward to this lesson!' or (not after you've read this chapter) 'Oh no, it's going to be a long hour'. Getting the lesson starter right can inspire the children from the word 'go' and thus also keep any behavioural problems to a minimum. It really can make that much difference. The flexibility that starters allow for means you can introduce new learning, consolidate previous learning, revise or practise important skills, or make links from previous lessons.

Getting the beginning of your lesson right, through the inventive use of a starter, can really set your lesson up well. Link it with the rest of your lesson (if possible) and try to keep away from just run-of-the-mill question-and-answer sessions. They really just don't cut it. Be careful, also, of activities projected on your interactive whiteboard; as great as some of the games may be, as fun as the children might find them, having one or two children playing a game and 28 looking on really isn't very good. Not only does it throw up possibilities for behaviour issues, it's also not promoting that personalized all-inclusive lesson that we all want. So, unless you can play one of those games and involve every other child in the class, I would steer clear.

## Getting started on starters!

What kind of things should you be doing then? Well your lesson starter needs to:

◆ inspire your pupils so they become involved in your lesson from the outset, and
◆ be appropriately differentiated so as to include all children.

And that's about it. So, without further ado, here's a (quite long) list of starters, many of which can be used for different lessons, some which are more lesson-specific.

*Mystery number game*

Write a number on the board and cover it with a piece of paper. Children then have to ask questions to work out what the number could be. Try to encourage mathematical language, such as the examples below.

◆ *Is it odd/even?*
◆ *Is it a multiple of ...?*
◆ *Does it have factors of ...?*
◆ *Is it larger/smaller than ...?*

You can also use this activity with words.

◆ *Is it a connective?*
◆ *Does it have two/three/four vowels?*
◆ *Does it have two/three/four syllables?*

*Fizz-buzz*

Get the children standing up. Give them a times table/multiple of, which they pass around the class. If the next number is on that times table they say 'Fizz'. Build it up by giving two times tables; if the number is on the other table they say 'Buzz'. If it's on both they say 'Fizz-buzz'. Here's an example.

◆ Start with the two times table.
◆ First child starts counting at '1', next child says 'fizz', '3', 'fizz', '5', 'fizz', etc.
◆ Add another times table – for example, 5
◆ '1', 'fizz', 3, fizz, 'buzz', 'fizz', '7', 'fizz', '9', 'fizzbuzz', etc.

*Steps*

In pairs or group, and with or without dictionaries, give the children a start word. The next word in the list has to start with last letter of the previous word, for example:

helpful – lovely – yoghurt.

To make it harder you could insist on a subject area or word type – for example, adjectives only.

*Spot the mistake*

Write a sentence on the board that has obvious mistakes, maybe linked to the objective you're covering. Wait to see if any children spot it before the lesson starts. If not, give them a gentle prod!

*Splat*

Splat is a great game loved by children of all ages. It's very simple. You choose four children, who stand up. You ask a question (probably works best in Maths but can be used in other subjects). The first child with the answer shouts it out, then has to shout 'Splat!'. This 'splats' the others and stops them answering. The child who is first to get it right remains standing and another three 'challengers' stand up for the showdown. Keep a record of which child manages the most consecutive 'wins'. Children *love* the competition and challenge, and it gives you an opportunity to revisit a particular area with the questions.

*Alien counting*

Explain that you will be using an alien form of counting in Maths today. Tell your pupils that each time you pat your shoulder that is a unit, each time you click your fingers that is a ten and if you pat your head that is a hundred. Use this technique to create a number – can they tell you what it is? This is a great technique for working on place value. Make it so they have to answer you the same way!

*Dense teacher*

Get the children to help you with a problem that you can't work out. They'll love the fact you can't do it and they can!

*Continuum*

Draw an imaginary line across the front of the room. Each end represents an opposing point of view. When looking at a persuasive or argumentative text, ask children before reading the text where they would put themselves, in terms of their opinion, on the line. Children place themselves at an appropriate point along this line, justifying their decision. This activity can be revisited as a plenary to see whether opinions have changed as a result of the lesson.

### Who am I?
Children stick the name of a character from a book on their forehead. They ask a partner questions about an element of this character to find out who they are. This can be done in pairs or by mingling throughout the classroom.

### Do it in three
Choose one child from each group to give a summary of a given learning objective or topic in exactly 3 minutes. Not a second more!

### There's a hole in my bucket
Ask the children to think about, and list, all the uses for a bucket with a hole in it.

### Eyes closed
Ask the children to close their eyes while you describe something to them. Then ask them to draw on their whiteboards what they think you are describing. For example:
   'I have a shape with five sides; it has one line of symmetry and two angles larger than 90 degrees.'

### Milling around
Everyone in the class walks around the room and, on a given signal, teams up with someone. In their pairs, they have 1 minute to describe to each other one thing they learned from a previous lesson.

### Show me!
This is a simple yet powerful technique for engaging the whole class. Each child has an individual whiteboard (the best resource ever!) and writes down the answer to any question you may ask. No one holds up their board until you say 'Show me!'.

### Draw it!
This activity works well as a plenary too. Ask the children to draw their learning from whichever lesson/topic you choose. They represent visually what they learned. This can be done as a diagram, or a mind map or a spider diagram – anything really that

helps them to remember. Don't place restrictions on this activity. The children then explain what they have done to their partner and listen to what their partner has to say before adding anything they've missed.

*Unscramble*
Write some key words on the board tied in to the lesson. Children have a set time to unscramble the words.

*Ask me*
Ask pupils to prepare two questions each that they would like answering about the previous lesson. They can do this on Post It® notes and stick on a wall/board for you or other children to answer later on.

*What was it?*
Write three answers on the board from previous learning. Ask the children if they can work out the questions.

*Beat the teacher*
Everyone (teacher included) has a mini-whiteboard and pen. Give a calculation, then you and your pupils start doing it. I either give them the time it takes me plus 1 minute, or set a timer on the inter-active whiteboard to do it. Children love it! It gives you instant feedback about how they are doing and it gives them competition to be the first with correct answer.

*Taboo*
Just like the famous board game ... In turns, a child chooses from a bag a term they have learned the previous lesson. They should attempt to describe the term to their classmates without using the word itself. Other children try to guess what the word is.

*Call my bluff*
Like the well-known TV show. Provide the children with a new word, concept or phrase. Give them three possible definitions. Children should work in pairs to decide which definition is correct. This could also work well as a plenary reviewing new vocabulary from the lesson.

*Show me variation*
This is a variation of Show me! from the previous category of activities, but this version takes a little longer to prepare. Children are

given ready-made cards and raise them in answer to questions or definitions given by the teacher in a 'most likely to' type of activity. Here are some examples.

◆ Children are given cards with words such as protein, carbohydrate, fat, etc. They raise the correct one when you call out a different type of food: beef, pasta, bread, chocolate, etc.

### KWL (Know already/Want to know/have Learned)

A KWL grid is a good way of helping to personalize children's learning; it's also a good way to begin a new topic. Children draw a three-column grid and fill in each column under the headings. The last column is completed at the end of the topic (see Table 10.1).

### Ordering

Children are given cards showing (in text or graphic form) key concepts relating to the topic to be covered in the lesson. They have to arrange them in what they think is the correct order of importance/chronology/characteristics, etc.

**Table 10.1 KWL grid**

| What I already know | What I want to know | What I have learned |
|---------------------|---------------------|---------------------|
|                     |                     |                     |
|                     |                     |                     |
|                     |                     |                     |

### Bingo

Use with numbers, words, pictures, etc. Children can choose their own numbers, but with words and pictures it's usually best to have something created in advance. This activity is not just to be used for maths – consider other areas of the curriculum, too!

### Find me a partner

Half the class are given questions and half are given answers. Children must silently move around the room trying to find out who their partner is. This activity could also be done with them talking, and the questions and answers being stuck on their backs to make it a bit more challenging. Alternatively, instead of questions finding answers, questions could find other questions that provide the same answer or answers could find other answers from the same times tables and then order themselves. Many different possibilities for this one!

### Number fans

Number fans are a great resource for quick mental maths starters. Google Number fans and you'll find plenty of templates to use. Just make sure that children hide their answers and all show you at the same time! Excellent for quick Assessment for Learning too.

### Up and down

Kids love this one and it causes lots of laughter in the classroom. Read from a piece of text and ask the children to listen out for a certain type of word – for example, an adjective. When they hear one they stand up; when they hear another they sit down. And so on. Works with all sorts of different word types, etc. (As an aside, we used to do this for a bit of fun when we had a couple of minutes to spare –except we used to do it to the song 'My Bonnie Lies Over the Ocean'. Every time there was a word beginning with 'B', the children stood up or sat down. Try it, causes mayhem, especially in the chorus! If you don't know the song, or have no idea what I'm talking about, just move on!)

Just remember that your lesson starter needs to be inspirational, appropriately differentiated and engaging.

So that's starters done with. There are many, many more of them and I could quite easily fill a book with these alone. That said, there is enough variety in this chapter to keep you going for a while. Many of the activities will work as plenaries too, so double value for your money!

# 11 Outstanding ... Plenaries

Well, you've started the lesson brilliantly, drawing all the children in, enthusing them with expectation. By using your quick AfL strategies you've grouped pupils and been able to focus their learning even more. Your fantastic questioning has led to some wonderful debate and the children are so engrossed they don't want the lesson to end. You look at your watch and realize that there's only a few minutes left; you've lost track of time. 'Ah, it doesn't matter; the children are having such a great time I won't stop them now. It's only the plenary; we can miss that off the end.' Stop. Right. There. Never, ever, ever, ever (ever) miss out your plenary. Ever. We'll have a look later what to do if the lesson time is shorter than you'd planned for whatever reason, but you must always include the plenary. (You could have a recap or plenary at any point during the lesson, not just at the end. Just make sure you do one!)

I dare say that you do a plenary most, if not all, of the time anyway. And this chapter will help you to make those plenaries outstanding, tying up your lesson perfectly and ensuring all the children know about the learning that has taken place. And, of course as a side issue, you won't get an outstanding grade if you don't have a plenary. Here we go then –aims of this chapter:

♦ to provide useful, detailed advice on how to plan and use plenaries effectively
♦ to offer loads of classroom strategies that exemplify the approaches suggested.

Best place to start then, right at the beginning.

## What is a plenary?

A plenary is that part of the lesson where pupils are made explicitly aware of the learning that has happened. This may sound a little ridiculous; surely they will know that from the teaching that has taken place? Of course they'll be aware of what the focus has been about through the objectives you've used and the success criteria they've been working with. What the plenary's job is, is to make crystal clear the vocabulary and objectives and bring it all together, reinforcing the children's learning. Yes, many children will have it cemented in their heads already; what you are doing is reinforcing for everyone and extending the thinking wherever possible. Let's look at four areas that we would want in an outstanding plenary: clarity, involvement, ability to apply and meta-learning.

**Clarity:** The key is that all the children are clear about what the main learning objectives. That doesn't necessarily mean they have to fully understand them, just that they are aware of what they are. A plenary provides the opportunity to take a small step back from the activity part of the lesson and think about their learning.

**Involvement:** Perfect if all children are involved! This doesn't mean that they all need to say something, or be asked a question, just that they are given the opportunity to reflect on their learning.

**Be able to apply:** The plenary provides an opportunity for the children to develop their learning independence (more personalized learning!). They could be encouraged to link to previous learning or think what future learning could be.

**Meta-learning (or learning about learning):** In order to make children real independent learners they need to develop and under-stand different strategies. They need to be made aware of these strategies and helped to use the vocabulary needed to vocalize them.

A plenary, therefore, can really help children to develop the skills they need in order to transfer their thinking skills to other contexts. And you just thought they were tagged on to the end of the lesson to tick a box. But it doesn't end there; there are other uses too (you didn't think you were getting off that lightly did you?) such as AfL and recognizing achievement.

**AfL:** Obviously, this was going to make an appearance! Asking children to clarify their learning or use in a new context will help to throw up any areas of misunderstanding or gaps in their learning. And we all know what we do with that information (and if you don't, read Chapter 5).

**Recognizing achievement:** Plenaries give you a great opportunity to celebrate children's learning, letting them know that you are proud of their achievements. And this will obviously reap benefits in all sorts of ways.

Many of the activities in Chapter 10 can very easily be adapted for use as a plenary. Likewise, many of the plenary activities here can be adapted for use as starters. But I'm not going to put both in both chapters; what a waste of time that would be!

### Five golden rules

This is a good way of getting children to determine what they think is most important about the learning in the lesson. In the plenary, they have to decide (working in groups probably works best for this) the top five rules (maximum) they would have to take from their learning in order to complete a similar task, for example:

◆ What are the top five rules for collaborative working?
◆ What are the top five rules in decision making?

### Testing a hypothesis

Give the children a statement of an explanation, concept, process, etc. In groups, they look at the statement and come to a consensus of whether they agree with it or not. They need to give opinions why. If wrong, what is wrong or how could it be changed? This is quite a challenging thing for them to attempt, especially for the first time. It can be differentiated quite easily by making the statement more or less complex. It is also more likely to be used after a series of lessons around a topic rather than just a single lesson. For example:

In order for a plant to grow healthily, it needs only water. Discuss.

### Mnemonics

These work very well, as I'm sure you're aware. Make sure the children have time to come up with a memorable one; this usually works best if they work in pairs or small groups – for example: spelling 'every', and remembering the planets (without Pluto!):

◆ *even vampires eat raspberry yoghurts*
◆ *most vexing experience, mother just served us nothing!*

### Pass it around

Give each pair of children a blank sheet of paper and remind them to put their names on it. In their pairs, they are given a problem to start working out an answer. After a set period of time they give their paper to another pair and receive a paper from a different pair. They then have a set time to redraft, answer and extend the work. They do this as many times as you think is reasonable. Eventually, they receive their own paper back which they work on to produce a final version.

### What have I learned?

The plenary is important because it forces children to distinguish between the key learning objectives you want and any extra information they may have encountered along the way. The following are fun ways to help that process and help the children to be able to summarize their thoughts and ideas clearly in a different context. Encourage them to use their own words and not just regurgitate the objectives verbatim. For example, using the example of a plant life cycle again:

◆ Newspaper headline: 'Plant comes for short town visit'. Write an exclusive.
◆ Persuasive argument: 'Plant life cycle is the best!' Discuss.
◆ Headstone: an orchid has died. What would be written on its headstone?

### Three things learned today

Ask pupils, working on their own, to list the three most important things they learned today. Then ask them to find out from a neighbour the three most important things *they* learned today.

### Diagrams

Ask pupils to draw a spider diagram showing what they have learned today. Or/And ask them to draw a mind map, showing the same thing. Make sure they explain their diagrams to a partner/ neighbour, adding anything they may have missed after a discussion.

### Question it!

Children write questions on Post-Its® at the beginning of the lesson after the learning objectives have been shared. They stick these notes on a designated board . The questions are answered by different children at the end of the lesson.

*Compose two*
Give the children 1 minute to compose two statements: one explaining what they have learned; and the other explaining how they have learned it. Then ask them to work in pairs to make the statements even better. Later, the all the children can share their statements with the whole class.

*Pyramid*
Give children a triangle that has been split into five horizontal sections. Ask them to place what they consider to be the five most important parts of the lesson into it. This can then form the basis for any discussion about what they had and why they considered this point to be more important than that point, etc. Again, this reinforces learning while simultaneously deepening understanding and thinking. I suggest laminating A4 sheets with pyramids on so whiteboard pens can be used and easily wiped off.

A variation on this could be ranking the points in terms of their understanding. A further variation could be using this activity over a series of lessons. Children have to have five points on the pyramid at all times, but rub out the ones they are secure with, replacing them with another one.

*Learning boards*
This idea can be used as a plenary over a few sessions. On a piece of paper, allow the children to design their own 'learning board', which they can add key information to as the lessons progress. They will eventually have a page filled with all their learning on that particular topic. Laminate them and they can then be used for reference as often as needed.

*Ready, steady, teach!*
This is a plenary activity that children love. Give them a set of materials (scissors, glue, paper, clay, etc.) and ask them to make a model that represents one key aspect of their learning from that lesson. But only give them a limited time to work in. This really focuses their thinking. As always, elicit information from them as to why they chose it, how they think it represents their learning, etc.

*Quiet sentences*
Group the children into fours. Each group receives a set of four envelopes. Each envelope contains part of a sentence, but none of the envelopes contains everything they need in order to make a full

sentence. So to make their sentences, they need to give each other words from their own envelopes. They have to do this in silence. Again, set a time limit to focus thinking. Review sentences afterwards, making sure the children give reasons for their choices.

### Concept cartoons

Concept cartoons have been around since the early 1990s and are a great way of engaging children in their learning. If you have never come across these, have a look at http://www.conceptcartoons. com. Basically, they are cartoons that contain different explanations for a concept or process. Only one of the explanations is correct; the others are based on children's popular misconceptions. This allows for fantastic questioning and discussion. Once you understand how these cartoons work (just use Google images for plenty of examples) you can create your own. And when the children understand how they work, *they* can produce *their* own – great personalized learning happening there: children thinking about their own, and each other's, misconceptions.

### Dominoes

A great plenary idea but it does take a bit of preparation. Prepare a set of dominoes with questions on one half and answers on the other. The question and answer on the same card don't match. Give out the cards to each pupil and invite one of them to ask a question. The child with the correct answer reads it out and then asks their question and so on. Children can then make their own sets to share with the class.

### Learning tree

This is a fantastic ongoing display and learning resource, best done over the course of a topic or series of lessons. Children are given leaves (no more than five) each lesson. In the plenary they have to record something they have learned on each leaf and stick it on a class display of a tree. Two great outcomes from this: children are constantly thinking about their learning to choose the most important parts; and over time it helps to build up the 'big picture' of learning for that topic. It's important that you, as the teacher, set out your tree according to the learning you want to promote. For example, you might be looking, in Science, at forces. You might decide to have four main branches on your tree: one each for gravity, mass and weight, balanced forces and unbalanced forces. The children could add their leaves to the particular branch you are focusing on any given lesson.

Fantastic whole-class resource and plenty of opportunities for the children to revisit their learning at any time.

### End-of-lesson reviews

At the start of the lesson, one child is appointed as 'rapporteur' (derived from an old French word, indicating someone who is appointed by a committee or board to investigate something and report back on it). You then teach your lesson as normal. Then, in the plenary, it is the job of the rapporteur to sum up the learning and report their findings back to the rest of the class. The rapporteur also takes questions from the class. If they can't answer them, they can ask other members of the class for assistance. What you will probably find is that after a very short time children are queuing up for the job! It is probably best introduced at the beginning of the year, or at the beginning of a new term, which is why it's in this category.

### Die plenary

Make a large cardboard die or stick pieces of paper onto each side of a large die you may already have. Each side will have a different statement as follows.

1 Ask the teacher a question about the learning in the lesson.
2 Ask someone else a question about the learning in the lesson.
3 Say what you found easiest in the lesson.
4 Say what you found most difficult in the lesson.
5 Say what you found most interesting in the lesson.
6 Say what you found most important in the lesson.

Give the die to different children and ask them to roll it. They then have to do whichever side faces upward.

## No time left?

OK, coming back then to what to do if the lesson timings go astray? We've all been there, starter goes over, lesson starts late, etc. But like I said earlier, do not lose the plenary. Instead, try these approaches.

◆ Shorten the time for the task, perhaps just get pupils half-way through with the expectation to finish another time. Make this clear to them (and anyone else who may be watching!) before going into your plenary. Remember, you need to go back over their learning.

◆ Cut an activity from the lesson, if you have other activities going on.

◆ Do the plenary in the lesson. Stop the children while they are doing their task and spend 10 minutes going over the learning. You can then let them continue with their task up until the end of the lesson. Always explain what you are doing 'We are going to stop there for a minute and review what we've learned so far. We'll do it now so as we have enough time to review it properly' – or something like that. This informs them, and, again anyone watching, that their learning is the most important thing.

## And so ...

The key thing to remember about any plenary is that the quality of questioning is what will bring about the greater thinking and, ultimately, understanding. Whichever activity you use, keep that in mind and you'll be producing outstanding plenaries in no time at all!

**Remember:**

◆ Revisit the learning objective.
◆ Review the success criteria.
◆ Always extend or challenge your children.

# 12 Outstanding ... Homework

Homework. Ah, one of the most controversial topics in the whole primary classroom. On the whole, teachers hate setting and marking it, children hate receiving it and parents/guardians hate doing it! It causes distress, heartache, feelings of helplessness, and no small amount of grumbling and moaning. And that's just teachers. You may get the odd(?) child who actually likes receiving homework, and you may have some parents who will ask you throughout the year if you can give their child more. However, as I'm sure you're aware, these are few and far between. It's more likely that you will get arguments along the lines of it disrupts family life, burdens the children too much, limits learning and puts children off school, especially when they haven't completed it on time. So why do we do it then? Why do we continue to give out homework week after week after week, knowing it will only cause grief, in one form or another, to everyone involved? That's a good question. And one that isn't so easy to answer. Your school no doubt has a homework policy, built on the assumption that homework actually helps to embed the knowledge taught during the week. As we've already seen, the best way to embed knowledge is to discuss, question and teach learning to and with others, not complete a wordsearch about Henry VIII's wives. So this is the approach *we're* going to take with homework (no, not the Henry wordsearch idea).

Let's have a look at the arguments in favour of homework first.

- ◆ Homework encourages parental involvement.
- ◆ The vast majority of schools have homework policies.
- ◆ Parents are in favour of schools setting homework even though they harbour concerns about how long it takes.
- ◆ Parents become involved in different ways: making sure it's completed; taking away any distractions so it can be completed; give assistance when needed.

♦ It helps to embed learning.
♦ It encourages independence.

And against ...

♦ It disrupts family life.
♦ It is biased in favour of more advantaged homes.
♦ It causes increased workload for teachers.
♦ Parental involvement doesn't always raise achievement; poorly educated parents can be disadvantaged by it.
♦ It doesn't help to embed learning; children just do it because they have to.

Some pretty strong arguments from both sides, but what about a solution? Well, I'm not climbing on my soapbox and starting my own election campaign in favour of one argument or another. What I *am* going to do is list some much better ways, in my opinion, of giving homework to your children that *will* help to embed their learning, or will help them in the classroom for future lessons. I will admit, though, to thinking that any homework that involves copying, colouring, finishing off or doing 'more of the same' should be dumped in the filing cabinet in the corner and disposed of at the first opportunity. Those kind of activities give homework a bad name; in fact they could well be what got homework its awful reputation in the first place!

One initiative that has been seen to work well is homework clubs/study centres. These can be effective if they are run during lunchtimes or after schools, and for some children this does have a positive impact. They don't seem to mind as much if they are doing their homework alongside friends, or even if they are still at school: work from school being done at school. Works very well if you can encourage parents to attend too.

However, this is something that can be done *after* the homework has already been set, but it doesn't really help us in thinking about ways of making homework seem more enjoyable for children. Your school may not want to run homework clubs or (indeed) you may not want to do one yourself, so this option wouldn't work in any case. Therefore, we need to explore ways of setting homework that don't cause everyone to mumble and grumble every time the word is mentioned! So, onto ...

## Homework with a purpose

Here we go then. Nothing in this chapter will have anything to do with giving out worksheets. No 'We've been practising column subtraction all week, so I want you to go home and practise some more; there are 20 questions on this sheet; you need to do them all.' Oh great. See the eagerness on those beautiful little faces when you pull this one on a Friday afternoon. Nope, none of this at all. The activities in the following pages are all focused on talking and learning. Occasionally you may be asking for them to write something down, but this will be as an aid to them rather than the whole point of the homework. Many of the questioning activities and activities in the starters and plenaries chapters (Chapters 10 and 11) can be adapted quickly as homework too. Let's get on with it then.

### Planning

I know, I know, this word has reared its ugly head again! Whatever homework you decide to give, don't just decide 5 minutes before you give it out and send someone off to the photocopier machine to get it sorted. It doesn't mean, though, that you have to spend ages planning it either. All I'm suggesting by planning is that you think in advance about what you want the homework to be; this will be beneficial with some of the types of homework mentioned here.

### Choice

I've put this area first as I think it could immediately have an impact on the children's perception of homework. Just having some choice will encourage more of them to want to do their homework, with little extra work needed on your part. Let the children decide how they want to present their homework to you. They may feel happier presenting it in lots of different ways. Obviously, the 'let's practise adding up' homework doesn't initially seem like it would fit this idea, but asking the children to find a different way of explaining their learning will result in them having to think deeper about the concept they have been taught, embedding that learning more. Providing children can explain their homework, however it may be presented, and they have explained the concept correctly, then surely the homework has done its job? That's the important part as far as I'm concerned. Here's a (not exhaustive) list of different ways of presenting homework.

- Making models.
- Writing a song about their learning.

- Doing a drama sketch.
- Writing a poem.
- Doing a PowerPoint presentation.
- Taking photographs to explain.
- Using illustrations.
- Making a collage.
- Doing a mind map.
- Making up a game.
- Writing a diary entry.
- Drawing a cartoon strip.
- Designing a leaflet or a poster.
- Interviewing someone.

Now link with these ideas and see what happens.

*Open objectives*
Set an objective as homework. Discuss with the children what the objective is going to be and let them investigate and present their findings in any way they want. You can even set it so they have to come into school ready to teach a 5-minute lesson based on the objective you've given them.

*Quiz*
Ask the children to prepare some questions on a topic that you have been studying ready for use in the next lesson. You can, if you want to extend it, ask them to complete it in the form of a quiz game. You will find that this is a great activity for assessment purposes too. Children will have to come up with the answers as well, obviously showing their depth of understanding.

*Decisions, decisions*
Give out some statements to the children based on what they have been learning. Ask them to rank these statements against set criteria that you provide. For example, ask them to put a set of statements about sentence construction in order of importance, with you giving the criteria about what a sentence must be.

*Reduce*
Choose a lesson or a series of lessons and ask the children to compress the things they have learned into three key points. When they come back with their statements, they need to be able to justify their decisions, explaining why they chose the ones they did and why they

chose to omit others. This can provide some fascinating discussion in the classroom, again giving you some opportunities to assess.

### Mark the teacher

Very few things give children as much pleasure as discovering their teacher has made a mistake. Give your pupils a piece of work that you have done. Tell them you are extremely proud of it and you want to show them how good it is. Then let them find all your mistakes. You'll have loads of kids waving pieces of paper under your nose Monday morning telling you how many mistakes you'd made!

### Ask at home

Children love asking questions. All we have to do is get them interested in asking questions about the stuff we want them to! Chapter 8 gives several examples of great ways to pose questions and lots of examples of how this can generate discussion. Think of an open-ended question and give it to the children to take home with them. Ask them to discuss the question with their parents/guardians or older siblings/relatives. This kind of activity produces some excellent responses in the lessons following. Many parents will enjoy discussing questions like this with their children and the children are eager to share this discussion back at school. Questions that invite opposite viewpoints work very well with this activity. You could set up a class blog and invite the children and their parents to contribute. This works well if you have a secure virtual learning environment through your school. Which leads us on to ...

### Virtual homework

By now, many schools will have a Virtual Learning Environment, also known as a Learning Platform. These can have a huge impact on the way homework is set for children. You can use learning platforms to:

◆ upload homework so children can access it from home; you can add website links, pictures, clipart, video links and so on if you want them to look at anything specific
◆ get children to upload their homework into their own work area from home
◆ set up online blogs or forums that children can use to discuss a given topic, along with their parents
◆ access wikis to enable children to build their own bank of resources and information.

### Homework rewards

You need to be careful about using rewards connected to homework – or any school work for that matter. Encouragement and praise need to be given in abundance, where suitable, but be aware that you want children to do things because they enjoy doing them, not because they're going to get something in reward, such as sweets or a pencil! There isn't anything wrong, though, with some encouragement and incentives. As an example, I did a display in my classroom called 'Read around America'. I had a big map of America on a display board and labelled about 40 cities. Each child had their name on a push-in pin, which they moved around the board every time they read a new book. Their home reading diary had to be signed by their parents to say they had read the book. It caused great competition and incentivized the children to read more at home. The fact they wanted to read more was as important at the time as what they were reading; I did allow them to read newspapers, magazines, etc. (although I drew the line at a takeaway menu!). Incentives do work well, but remember you really want children to do homework for the love of it.

### It's all about the talk

And the title says it all. I'm a firm believer in the best type of homework being the type that involves plenty of discussion. By making this the case you are also involving the adults at home, which helps the child again with their learning. Most children love discussing what they are learning at school, especially if it means they can teach their parents. I can't stress this highly enough – get them talking and you'll get them learning. Go through some of the activities here and use the questioning strategies talked about in Chapter 8. It's the questions that make the homework work:

Ask the question, get the talk at home, present it back at school = great learning!

# 13 Outstanding ... Support for TAs and LSAs

Teaching assistants (TAs), or Learning support assistants LSAs), or specialist teaching assistants (STAs), or behaviour support assistants (BSAs) or higher-levels teaching assistants (HLTAs) are just some of the extra adults working in our classrooms. Quite a few different names! There has been a big shift in the number of extra adults now employed in classrooms, there with the proviso of helping to raise the pupils attainment. Alongside the teacher, they have had to adapt themselves to the needs of a variety of pupils who come from an ever-changing multicultural society. What may well have been appropriate in the classroom ten years ago is unlikely to be so today. Your job as the teacher is to make optimum and innovative use of all the adults working in your classroom – which can be a difficult management issue, especially for the inexperienced teacher. It can often mean you are moved out of your comfort zone and required to change your thinking and teaching, making it one of the most demanding of challenges.

Since 2003, there has been a continually evolving workforce in schools underpinned by a new professional framework for HLTAs. Every school now has the opportunity to develop its staff according to its own needs and priorities. There is a range of additional staff now working in schools with roles and responsibilities as varied as the schools from which they come. Successful schools have used these varying types of extra adults to support the learning needs of the children in their care. Teaching assistants have been seen as vital in developing these news ways of learning within the classroom. Knowing that children need differing levels of support at different times to suit their individual needs has led to teaching assistants being integral to the progress made in classrooms, with the best classroom practice involving teaching assistants in much of the planning process. This also means that teachers can more easily begin to address some of the issues around personalized learning that can, perhaps, be difficult without added adult support.

The teaching assistant's role has changed in recent years. There is a huge cultural shift happening in schools now around the most effective use of these staff. And the schools embracing this change are the ones finding the most benefits. Gone are the days of a TA sitting next to one child in the class whispering in their ear explanations of what the teacher is saying; now they are at the forefront, alongside the teacher, of new and innovative teacher-led activities that are only just being explored. This new teamwork approach can reap many, many dividends; not least the accelerated progress of the children.

A lot to think about then! But fear not! Through this chapter we will address some of the issues and provide you with ideas to help make fantastic use of what can be a wonderful resource!

## How quality of teaching can be improved

A teaching assistant, working as part of a team dedicated to learning and teaching, can substantially improve the quality of teaching. In order to be an outstanding teacher you need to show you can make outstanding use of any extra support you may have in your classroom. Teaching is improved when the teaching assistant:

◆ works in close partnership with the teacher, made obvious through the planning, and has good arrangements in place with the teacher for monitoring and feeding back on children's behaviour and learning
◆ is knowledgeable enough to extend children's learning
◆ has good questioning skills
◆ interacts with the teacher to make the lesson more lively or create discussion
◆ deals with minor behaviour issues, enabling the teacher to carry on teaching the whole class
◆ helps the teacher to organize groups so as to more closely match the ability of the children to the work set.

Let's look at these areas in more depth.

### Close partnerships
In order to have a partnership with your TA, you need to include them in everything you possibly can. But most of all value them. And

tell them so. Lots. They can help make your life so much easier and really help to push the learning of the children.

Include them in your planning as much as possible. If it's not possible to spend some time with them during the time you plan – and it's definitely worth asking your senior managers if your TA can come out of the classroom for half-hour or so during your PPA (planning, preparation and assessment) – then make sure you find some time for their input. This can be as simple as a 'working lunch' in the classroom (I know this isn't ideal, but you will find that your TA will love the fact that you value their opinion and make sure you supply the biscuits/cake/chocolate, etc.), or even something more simple. Quickly jot down your thoughts on your planning for the following week, give them to your TA, and ask if they can have a look and come back to you with any ideas or suggestions for anything particular for specific children. (There's more on this later in the chapter.)

Find time (5 minutes at any point during the day) to ask for their feedback on any learning for any child they've been working with. Support sheets work well here. Make a very quick tick sheet (with some room for comments) for use during the week, with space for learning objectives, success criteria and so on for your TA to use during lessons. When you are doing your assessment for learning stuff (and you know where to find all that useful info!), a quick nod in the direction of your TA will allow them to record any child who isn't confident with their learning on that concept, and allow you to do something about it later. This is outstanding classroom practice, and really shows anyone observing how closely you and your TA are working. Not to mention the obvious benefit to the kids.

*Planning together*
If you are able to plan together, try to include these areas in your discussions.

◆ Learning objectives and success criteria. Discuss how you will use these and what activities you will be using to secure the learning outcome you desire.
◆ Discuss your role, and the role of your TA, in the lesson. Is there anything you want them specifically to do at a given time? Any questions to ask?
◆ Discuss the learning of any particular children (special needs or otherwise). What help can your TA give to help with this?
◆ Barriers to learning. What are these/what could they be, and how can they be overcome?

### Knowledge and questioning

In order to forward the learning of the children, your TA needs to have decent subject knowledge. If it's something they're not as confident about, then it's your job to help them. Supply them with material that will improve their knowledge; make sure you give them plenty of time to brush up on it too, so that means planning given to them well in advance. Ensure they are aware of how important quality questioning is; give them this book and ask them to look at Chapter 8! You will be surprised at the difference that will make.

### Interaction

This shows how well you and your TA get on, as well as showing how well you work together. Let your TA know you value their opinion and encourage them to share that opinion with you and the class during the lesson. Encourage them to ask questions (even if, in the early days of trying this, you prompt them with the questions you want them to ask and when!).

Involve your TA whenever you can. Ask them questions during the lesson.

♦ 'What do you think of that point, Mrs Smith?'
♦ 'Is there anything you would like to add?'
♦ On a nod from them: 'Is there someone from your group who has a good point to make?'

You could ask your TA to scribe for you on the board while you continue questioning the class (this can be beneficial if you have any behaviour issues that may arise when you turn your back!), again making sure you always include their thoughts too.

### Have a laugh!

Never underestimate the value of humour in your classroom. Even if being observed, don't feel that you can't include your TA in any light-hearted moments, especially if that's what you would normally do. It shows the observer how good your relationship is and lets them know that this is normal classroom practice.

### Dealing with behaviour

The number of adults working in today's classroom may have detrimental effects on some children's behaviour. What you need to establish, from the word 'go', is that for the purposes of behaviour management all adults working in the classroom should have the role of behaviour manager. Be explicit with your TA what about your expectations; ensure these expectations are fully understood by the TA and that they can/will follow them. The TA, as much as you, is a role model and should carry some responsibility to proactively manage the behaviour of children. If you do not agree on these guidelines and roles, and make them quite clear to the children too, problems can arise, as these examples show.

**Child:** 'You can't tell me what to do; you're not the teacher!'

**Teacher:** 'Why isn't the TA intervening here? It would make my job much easier.'

**TA:** 'Is it my job to intervene? Should I get involved?'

These situations can lead to confusion and difficulties. And, knowing how children can be, there will certainly be some who will try to play off one adult against another. So make this all clear from the outset. You might want to use some of the following to help remind you and your TA.

◆ Be aware of classroom rules and ensure a consistent approach.

◆ Make sure your TA, even if only assigned to one child, shares some of the responsibility for classroom behaviour management.

◆ Let your TA know they can use reward and sanction systems as appropriate.

The role of the teaching assistant is an ever-expanding one, and it is your job, as their line manager, to ensure they have the opportunity to make the best possible difference in that role. Share with them everything you feel is needed for them to do their job effectively; remember, it is your responsibility for this to happen. In your classroom, you are responsible for all the adults who work within it.

Teaching assistants can reduce your workload and stress levels as well as improving what goes on in the classroom. They can also be an invaluable help with AfL by tracking and monitoring specific children while you teach. By following these guidelines, you will be able to maximize the potential of the extra adults in the room, make and keep those great relationships and ensure that your children get the best possible support. Oh, and you'll tick that outstanding box too, but ...

**Remember:**

You must be showing that you are making outstanding use of your teaching assistant during all aspects of your lesson. They should *never* just be sitting and/or watching you. Involvement is key.

# 14 Outstanding ... Self-Evaluation and CPD

In order to become an outstanding teacher, you need to know first where you are at the moment and then, obviously, where you need to go next. The preceding chapters in this book can tell you where to go next; but it's up to you to audit where you are currently. Once you've done this, and then become outstanding, it's all about staying there. More on that in the final chapter.

Self-evaluation can be difficult; it becomes much easier when you're totally honest about it. You have to sit down, maybe with a glass of your favourite tipple (only one mind), and go through every part of your teaching giving yourself an honest critique about how good you think you are. Don't share it with anyone else at this point, just yourself. (There's an example of a checklist on my website listed at the end of this book.) Once you've done this you'll have a good idea of where you need to go next, sort of Assessment for Learning for teachers. Obviously, depending on what you feel you need to improve, the journey to outstanding may take a little while; it certainly won't happen overnight whatever stage you're at. I can honestly say, though, it is possible to get there. I went from being graded satisfactory to being outstanding in the space of one term. I'm not telling you that so I can blow my own trumpet, but to show you that *it is possible*. That said, you have to start with an honest assessment of your own practice. Take a look back over recent lesson observations, or Performance Management observations; look at the feedback you've been given. You may not agree with all of it; in fact you may think it's all nonsense. However, it's highly unlikely that your Head will have got it wrong by a large amount. You'll probably find they're pretty much spot on. And that's where you need to be honest with yourself and perhaps agree with them. Then work on the next steps to make improvements. Because, to be honest – and this may sound harsh – if you stop wanting to improve, stop wanting to get better for the difference it can make to the children in your class, then it's time to move on.

So, I've done the self-evaluation. What next? After reading this book cover to cover, taking out the bits you need, introducing them to your class and continuously trying to develop and improve them, you will be an outstanding teacher. But that doesn't mean you don't want to improve. And rightly so. We're going to have a look at the different ways you can get some brilliant CPD (continuing professional development), and many of them are right under your nose. In your own school. It's a common misconception that you only get great CPD by 'going on a course'. Yes courses do have their place, and I have to say I've been lucky enough to bear witness to some truly inspiring talks by very knowledgeable people. I've also been on some dross where, if everyone wasn't already asleep, they've been desperate for the afternoon coffee break so they can stock up on massive amounts of caffeine to stop the inevitable nodding off likely to occur. Do you want to take the chance of wasting a day out on a course delivered by someone who may not have seen the inside of a classroom since slate was last in fashion? No, I thought not.

### Peer mentoring and coaching

Mentoring and coaching is a great way of developing your practice. Some schools run a coaching and mentoring process whereby they tell you what you need to be working on with a colleague. The best relationship for development is when you decide what you need to improve on and work with someone who is good in that area. I suggest you look at people in your school and decide who is good at something you'd like to become better at, and then approach them to see if you can work alongside each other for a term. Watch them teach, if possible, or just talk with them about how they approach the area you're interested in. This will give you some great ideas for your development.

### AST/lead teachers

Most local education authorities use Advanced Skills Teachers and some have a lead teacher programme. It's always worth getting in touch with whoever co-ordinates this for your authority and ask if you can go to observe a lesson. If you give them an idea of an area you are interested in they will try to match you with someone who has strength in that area. Use them; they are a great resource.

*Learning walks*

If you've never come across learning walks before, then you're missing out! Basically, a learning walk is where you 'walk' around the school, on a given day at a given time, and drop in to other teachers' classes for a few minutes to watch what's going on. A lot of the time you'll have a focus to look for in every classroom – for example, engagement of children. It's a fantastic way of picking up little nuggets that you can take back and use in your own classroom. It is important, however, to remember that this is an opportunity for you to focus on good practice.

*Observing each other*

You can do this alongside mentoring and coaching, or just do it on its own. Take the opportunity to let other staff watch you teach; in fact, invite them to do so! In the same way as getting the children to teach a concept works (see Chapter 4), so will this. Choose something you want to improve on and make that the observed focus for the lesson. Ask staff to come and look at that area and give you honest feedback. This requires a little bravery on your part, but it's well worth the outcome. If you have the opportunity, watch other members of staff teach too. Again, it's a great way of acquiring new knowledge.

*Performance Management*

I know, not many of us like Performance Management! However, it can be a fantastic tool for your professional development. Discuss with your reviewer what you would specifically like to improve upon. It always works better if you can go in with an idea of how you could make that work. For example, if you said that you'd like to improve your behaviour management strategies and you knew that Miss Johnson was excellent at behaviour management, say this in your review. It will show that you've done your homework and you are clear about what you want to improve upon – always a good sign – and by having a ready-made solution for your reviewer it makes it more likely they'll agree to it happening; they don't have to do any of the thinking, you see!

*Schools sharing good practice*

This, in my opinion, is a vastly underused resource. There is good practice in every school in the country, even if it doesn't appear that way at first glance. Make use of schools in your area by getting in touch and asking if you can set up some way of sharing good practice (this may have to go through your Head; always a good idea to check first). In fact, it can be used as a whole school idea; I know of many schools that use this very effectively, even to the point of . . .

### Teacher swaps

The good practice outlined in the previous section can be further enhanced by teacher swapping. This is where a teacher from one school swaps with a teacher from a different school for a lesson, a day, a week or, in some cases, even longer. It's a superb way of gaining experience in a different setting, with different children, and it really can get you thinking about your own practice and how it can be improved. What works well in one school doesn't necessarily work as well in another, and vice-versa. Feedback sessions between the teachers after the event are hugely helpful and can really give some effective CPD opportunities.

### Have a student

Student teachers can vary vastly from one to another: some can be fantastic, looking like they've been teaching forever; and some can be not so good! Wherever possible, volunteer to have a student teacher for one of their placements. What this will mean is that you have to be on your toes all the time. The student teacher will have their set of standards that they need to show evidence they've achieved, and so will be looking to you for guidance on how they can achieve them. One of the ways they will be doing this is to watch good classroom practice. You will have to be thinking about your teaching every lesson in order to give them the best example possible. Having a student teacher can be extra work, but there is a great reward in the fact that it makes you evaluate your teaching too.

### Ask your TA/LSA

Never be afraid to ask. Everyone in your classroom will have an opinion on your teaching! Granted, they may not always share that with you but they'll have one nonetheless. So ask them. Talk to your TA about what they think of your classroom practice – for example, how they think you manage Assessment for Learning and what ideas they have for how it could be improved. Again, it can be a brave thing to do but it can help you to develop things you may not have been aware of. And then there's . . .

### Asking the kids

This one is a brave one too! Ask the children in your class what you do that helps them learn well; then ask what you could do better to help them learn even more. You will be surprised what they tell you. You could do this in the form of a short questionnaire, which will avoid any (possible) embarrassment if you do it as a whole-class discussion – you know how sometimes children aren't the most diplomatic! Having said that, it is very rare that they will be damning, but they will be honest. Try it.

## Teachers TV
An underused resource by many, but there is some great classroom practice on the website www.teachers.tv. You will find information on all areas of teaching and there is some great stuff on CPD too. Well worth a look. It's only available on the website now; the television programme no longer exists.

## Reading
Try to keep up with all the new initiatives that come out. It can be difficult, and tiresome at times, but it is important that you are aware of where things may be going. If you have an interest in one particular area, it's always worth approaching publications to see if they would be interested in you writing an article for them. This is another great way of you continuing to develop your practice.

## Staff meetings
Not always the most thrilling of hours spent in school, but they can be another way of improving practice. Listen to what anyone else may be saying about development courses they may have been on and, if appropriate, follow up this information with further discussion with the member of staff involved. You may find a little gem of an idea to use in your classroom and that's all you need to set you going again on the road to improvement!

## Classroom visits
Not in a formal way, like the learning walk, but as an informal 'pop-in' after school. Not just as a 'chat' session, but as a 'guided tour' (if you like) of the classroom, looking at specific areas in the room or at displays, etc. Ask the member of staff if they mind doing this; you can pay back the favour obviously, and you can pick up some great ideas this way. Approach your senior leadership team and ask if this is something you could do as a staff meeting, where you get guided tours of each other's classrooms. Plenty more development opportunities here.

From all these ideas you can see that there are plenty of opportunities to develop your practice without going out on courses, which (obviously) cost the school money! You've also got more chance of your Head saying 'yes' to an idea that could improve practice for a member of staff without costing them anything. It's important to keep wanting to improve your practice and by following some of the ideas here you undoubtedly will.

# 15  Becoming Outstanding and Staying Outstanding! Further Reading and Resources

Every child in every classroom the world over has the right to an education. It would be fantastic if that was an outstanding education. It's difficult to hit those high spots in your teaching regularly, but you've taken that first step towards it and bought this book, and hopefully by now begun to implement some of the ideas within it. There is a certain satisfaction that comes from knowing that you've improved yourself and your classroom practice, and the children in your class will be enjoying their learning more as well. And don't be afraid to tell everyone! Schools thrive on the enthusiasm of their staff – so be that enthusiastic teacher and share all your newly-found knowledge and outstanding practice (or, at the very least, give them the ISBN of this book!).

There will no doubt be times where your fantastic new learning strategy, the one that you've been planning for weeks, falls flat on its face. It's happened to all of us, don't worry about it. Put it in the 'OK so it didn't work' category and move on, maybe trying it again in a different way. Look at it from a different angle. Use that reflectivity to change, improve and adapt things to fit you and your classroom. Outstanding lessons are about taking risks, so never be afraid to take them! I was being observed by an OFSTED inspector and it came to the point, just before the activity, where I was grouping the children according to their self-assessment. All was going well and I was feeling pretty good about it. They came to move to their groups and suddenly, I realized that not only were there not enough chairs in the area I'd sent them to, but not enough tables either! Children were coming up to me saying that they didn't have anywhere to sit, and I could feel the panic rising. I looked over towards the inspector – not a sign of anything on his face; totally impassive. We quickly grabbed some tables from the other part of the room and carried them over to where they were needed. That's it, I thought. All aspirations of an outstanding lesson flew out of the window. It had taken much, much longer to get them into their groups than normal (I'd not counted the number of children in each group like I normally did, and sent them to areas accordingly), the pace of the lesson had dropped and it looked a shambles! But I was wrong. An outstanding judgement it was. So I asked the inspector 'How come?' I was convinced that all the hassle had ruined things. He said that although it wasn't as smooth a movement to groups as it could have been, the benefit the children got from working in a group that was specific to their learning needs far outweighed the extra couple of minutes it took to get them there. So don't be afraid. Take those risks and go with what you believe in; it will pay you back many, many times over.

Remember that when it comes to outstanding teaching and learning, it is never good luck over good planning. Also remember that you *will* be observed, by your senior management and possibly by OFSTED inspectors too (unless you plan your career to move to a new school that has very recently been inspected just before yours is due – and keep this cycle going). Although, with the new OFSTED framework, if you're in an outstanding school you won't be inspected for a minimum of five years from your last inspection, unless something flags up a worry. So no need to be too concerned. You don't need to go overboard on the planning and resources for your lesson, just keep saying to yourself: outstanding outcomes; what do I need to do so that *every* child in that lesson shows progress? That certainly won't happen because you have made some really colourful, fantastic, laminated cards for use in your starter that kept you up till 1 in the morning. It *will* happen if you know where your children are and where you need to take them next.

So now that you're outstanding, where next? You could just bask in the glory and think that you'd made it. All the hard work you put in had paid off and you're there. No more work needed. And obviously, that's not the answer you're going to get from me. Think about ways in which you can continue to improve, how you can pass on your knowledge, offer opportunities to other members of staff, maybe from other schools, to show good practice. Your local education authority could help out here. Also, there's the Advanced Skills Teacher route. Well worth looking into if that's where you feel you'd like to go next. It's hard work, and a whole day (yes, a whole day!) of assessment from external moderators, but well worth the time invested. There's more information here: www.teachernet.gov.uk/professionaldevelopment/ast/

You will find updated information, some resources and lots of other interesting stuff(!) at my website here: www.outstandingteaching.com

Here's a list of books (not exhaustive by any means) that I would recommend if you get chance. They will extend your thinking and provide you with new avenues to explore.

*Assessment for Learning*
**Active Learning Through Formative Assessment** by Shirley Clarke
   **Assessment for Learning: Putting it into Practice** by Paul Black, Chris Harrison, Clare Lee and Bethan Marshall
   **Putting Assessment for Learning into Practice (Ideas in Action)** by David Spendlove
   **The Assessment and Learning Pocketbook (Teachers' Pocketbooks)** by Ian Smith and Phil Hailstone

*Thinking skills*
**100+ Ideas for Teaching Thinking Skills (100+ Ideas) (Continuum One Hundred)** by Stephen Bowkett
   **Mind Maps For Kids: An Introduction** by Tony Buzan
   **Mind Maps for Kids: Max Your Memory and Concentration** by Tony Buzan
   **Thinking and Learning Skills Ages 5–7 (Creative Activities For …)** by Mike Fleetham, Lynne Williams and Andy Keylock
   **Thinking and Learning Skills Ages 7–11 (Creative Activities For …)** by Mike Fleetham, Linda Jones and Moreno Chiacchiero
   **Games for Thinking (Stories for Thinking)** by Robert Fisher
   **Poems for Thinking (Stories for Thinking)** by Robert Fisher
   **Stories for Thinking** by Robert Fisher

*Questioning*
**Questioning in the Primary School (Successful Teaching)** by E. C. Wragg and George A. Brown
   **Quality Questioning: Research-Based Practice to Engage Every Learner** by Jackie A. (Acree) Walsh and Elizabeth (Beth) D. (Dankert) Sattes

*Classroom management*
Behaviour Needs – www.behaviourneeds.com
   And there we are! And good luck!

# Index